The
Tarantula
in
My Purse

Photo by Ellan Young

WRITTEN AND ILLUSTRATED BY
JEAN CRAIGHEAD GEORGE

The Tarantula in My Purse

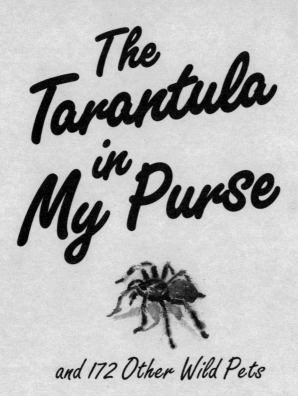

and 172 Other Wild Pets

A TRUMPET CLUB SPECIAL EDITION

ISBN 0-590-36321-2

Copyright © 1996 by Jean Craighead George. All rights reserved. Published by Scholastic Inc., 555 Broadway, New York, NY 10012, by arrangement with HarperCollins Children's Books, a division of HarperCollins Publishers. TRUMPET and the TRUMPET logo are registered trademarks of Scholastic Inc.

12 11 10 9 8 7 6   8 9/9 0 1 2/0

Printed in the U.S.A.   40

First Scholastic printing, November 1997

To Twig, Craig, and Luke

Contents

The Genesis

My children, Twig, Craig, and Luke, were the third generation of Craighead children who brought home wild birds and beasts to have and to contemplate. In their grandfather's day, and even in mine, wild animals were considered pests. There was no need for permits to keep them, as there is today. Hawks, owls, and falcons were shot. Crows and coyotes were poisoned. Songbird nests were raided for eggs. Anyone was free to bring home the earth's creatures to nurture and think about—and bring them home we did.

My father had started the tradition. He had lined his room with bottles of insects, raised snakes, and fed treats to a friendly skunk in the meadow. When called upon to dress up in his hated, lace-trimmed Lord Fauntleroy suit to go to town with his mother, he teased his wild friend until she sprayed him—to his delight. When he arrived at the back door, his mother ordered him to stay home and not come inside the house all day. So he didn't. Eyes sparkling, he fished the creek that ran through the backyard of his Pennsylvania home, caught frogs, ate dinner on the back porch, and stayed out until bedtime. How he loved that skunk.

When Frank and John, my twin brothers, and I were young, Dad encouraged in us that love of animals innate in all children. He found us walking sticks and assassin bugs, praying mantises, opossums, snakes, and owls. He taught us the plants they lived with and the environments where they could be found. To Dad all birds, beasts, and plants were works of art.

I must have learned this early. My first pet was a baby turkey vulture, a carrion eater fit for witches and monsters and associated with graveyards and death. He was a work of art. I loved him on sight.

Nod was about the size of a chicken and covered—all but his neck, head, and feet—with fluffy white down. His featherless head hung between protruding shoulders. He resembled a gargoyle on the Cathedral of Notre Dame.

Dad had found him sitting in the middle of a footpath in the Potomac River bottomlands near our home in Washington, D.C. The vulture had greeted him with a rasping hiss. Seeing no parents

anywhere, Dad put the gawky chick in his pack and brought him home to me.

Dad was an entomologist, but he did not concentrate on insects alone. He studied the whole forest or an entire ecosystem to find explanations for the behavior of a beetle or a wasp. He spent as much time as possible outdoors. The answers were all out there, he would say, not in books or at a desk. My mother, my brothers, and I went with him. He taught us the plants and animals and why birds migrate. He taught us how to hunt and fish, to make shelters and fire, but primarily he infused in us an enthusiasm for the ingenuity of nature.

No sooner had Dad put Nod in my hands than I hugged the awkward baby and asked what kind of a nest he had come from. That was a standard question in our household when new forms of life came to visit.

"A hollow log on the ground or the foot of a big tree," he answered.

"And what does he eat?"

"Carrion—dead things. Turkey vultures are the forest's sanitation department."

After Dad had fed him bites of a catfish he had caught in the Potomac River that day, I put a cardboard box on its side and lined it with newspaper. Nod waddled into it. I carefully pushed him under the kitchen table, then crawled in beside the box. He looked sideways at me out of bluish eyes set in wrinkled gray-blue skin. I patted his naked cheeks, and he sank to his heels. He closed his eyes and slept.

Nod throve on all manner of meat and fish, cooked and raw, and presently he was two feet tall with nearly six feet of wingspan. Mother grew nervous. When he flapped, her recipes flew across the room and flour puffed up from the cake-mixing bowl. This took her from nervousness to protest. Dad suggested we put Nod on the top of the kitchen door, where he could exercise without rearranging the kitchen.

High overhead he gave his full attention to Mother. His primordial instincts made him concentrate on her for two reasons. Turkey vultures roost together at night because they are safer in a group, and—the best reason—in the morning the young can follow experienced elders to food. Mother was Nod's elder. She brought chickens, roasts, and fish to the kitchen table. He followed her with his eyes from sink to stove to table.

Although Mother was also a naturalist, she was primarily a mother and the maestro of life in our home.

"Jean," she said one day, "Nod has to go. I can't stand a turkey vulture watching me cook another minute."

My father called his friend, the director of the National Zoo in Washington, D.C., and they made arrangements to ship Nod to a zoo in Scotland that did not have an American turkey vulture. When he was taken away, I cried until Dad pointed out that I had come to know a truly remarkable creature. Indeed I had.

When I grew up, I went right on bringing wild animals home; and when I had children, they did too. . . .

In the 1970s I was required to get a license to keep migratory birds and some of the mammals. That was an exciting event. For the first time in the history of humankind laws were passed to protect nature.

This book contains some of the stories about the 173 wild pets that taught me and my children so much about ourselves and the world.

CHAPTER 1

The Screech Owl Who Liked Television

Twig's favorite pet was a small gray screech owl. Had he not fallen from his nest before he could fly, he would have lived in the open woodland, deciduous forest, park, town, or river's edge. But he had landed on a hard driveway instead and ended up in our house. He was round eyed and hungry. He looked up at Twig and gave the quivering hunger call of the screech owl. Twig named him Yammer.

Yammer quickly endeared himself to us. He hopped from his perch to our hands to eat. He rode around the house on our shoulders and sat on the back of a dining-room chair during dinner.

Before the green of June burst upon us, Yammer had become a person to Twig, who felt all wild friends were humans and should be treated as such.

Wild animals are not people. But Twig was not convinced. One Saturday morning she and Yammer were watching a cowboy show on television. They had been there for hours.

"Twig," I said, "you've watched TV long enough. Please go find a book to read, or do your homework." My voice was firm. I kept the TV in my bedroom just so the children wouldn't be constantly tempted to turn it on as they had when it was downstairs.

Reluctantly, Twig got to her feet. At the door she turned and looked at her little owl. He was on top of the headboard, staring at the screen. A rider on a horse was streaking across the desert. From an owl's point of view the pair were mouse sized.

"How come Yammer can watch TV and I can't?" she asked, pouting.

Hardly had she spoken than Yammer pushed off from the headboard, struck the prey with his talons, and dropped to the floor, bewildered.

Twig rushed to his rescue. She gathered him up and hugged him to her chest. With a scornful glance at me, she hurried to her room. The small owl's round yellow eyes were peering from between her gently curled fingers.

Twig was right: This otherworldly creature was a person. Wasn't his menu of mice and crickets included on the shopping list? Didn't he have his own bedroom in the gap between the Roger Tory Peterson field guides in the living-room bookcase? Didn't he run down into the cozy blanket-tunnels made by Twig at bedtime and utter his note of contentment? And didn't he like TV just as she did?

Most scientists are taught not to read human emotions into animals, but sometimes they wonder about the truth of it. When you live with animals, they often seem quite humanlike.

Later that morning of the TV incident, I looked in on Twig and Yammer. The owl was perched on the top of her open door, preening his

feathers. She was sitting with her chin in her hands, looking at him.

"I feel sorry for Yammer," she said. "He's stuck in this house. He needs to see things that move like they do in the woods."

"So?" I said.

"So, I've finished my homework and made my bed. Can Yammer and I watch TV?"

I heard myself whisper, "Yes."

CHAPTER 2

Letting Yammer Go

When I told Twig she could watch TV that day of the cowboy incident, she stood on her desk and held up her hand to Yammer. He stepped onto her finger. As she climbed down, she touched his toes and the talons curled around her forefinger.

"I wish I had Yammer's feet," she said. "Then I could sit on the teeny tiny branches of the apple tree."

Suddenly her brother Craig shouted, "*Road Runner's* on."

"Yammer loves *Road Runner*," Twig said, and dashed to the TV in my bedroom. Yammer flapped his wings to keep his balance, and the two joined Twig's brothers, Craig and Luke, before the television. Luke, not quite four, patted the pillow next to him.

"Put him here," he said. A chord of music sounded, lights flashed, and all eyes—particularly

Yammer's—were riveted on that zany bird running on and off the screen.

Second to *Road Runner* was Yammer's love for the shower. He would fly into the bathroom when he heard one of us turn on the spray, sit on the top of the shower-curtain rod to orient himself, then drop into the puddles at our feet. Eyes half closed, he would joyfully flip the water up and into his wings and dunk his breast until he was soaked. A wet screech owl is as helpless as an ant in an ant lion's trap. Having bathed, Yammer couldn't climb out of the tub. We would have to pick him up and put him on a towel by the hot-air vent to dry.

This was a perfectly satisfactory arrangement until we failed to tell a visitor about Yammer's passion. In the morning, unaware of his quiet presence, she showered, stepped out of the tub, and left him there. It was almost noon before we discovered him.

Craig promptly put up a sign: "Please remove the owl after showering." It hung over the shower faucets for as long as Yammer lived with us.

Yammer was devoted to Twig. He sat on her shoulder at breakfast, flew to her hand for food when she whistled for him, and roosted on the window-curtain rod of her room when he was not watching TV.

He did like Craig's train set, however.

He had reason to. It moved like a garter snake. The tracks that Craig balanced on his big wooden blocks ran under the bed, then out across the floor past the chest of drawers, over the main line, and back under the bed again. When Yammer heard the train start up, he would fly to the back of the chair in Craig's room. Crouched to drop on this prey, he watched engine and cars ply the precarious route. The blocks would shudder as the little black locomotive swung around a curve or speedily crossed a ravine into the open stretch between the wall and the door. Yammer never struck this prey. The train was not the right size. Yammer was programmed to eat mice, insects, small snakes, and arthropods. The big owls, like the great horned, barred, and barn owls—pets of my childhood—might have pounced on Craig's train, but not Yammer. He just sat and watched. In a house that lacked diving blue jays and scurrying chipmunks, "Black Darling," as Craig called the Lionel train, was biological diversity to Yammer. His head fairly spun off his shoulders as his eyes followed the speeding engine around the room, under the bed, and out again.

Often the train wrecked. Craig ran it on the bleeding edge of disaster, and when the building blocks shifted too much, Black Darling would jump the tracks, knock down the trestles, and career through the air before coming to rest on its side, wheels spinning. With every crash, Yammer took off for Craig's door top, where he would study the dead engine until its wheels stopped turning. Then he would look away. When the train didn't move, it wasn't there.

One evening, a screech owl's plaintive call of spring floated through our windows as we were going to sleep. The voice came from the spruce trees on the other side of the lane.

The next day at breakfast I put down my fork and leaned toward Twig, Craig, and Luke, smiling. They put down their forks and looked at me with that oh-boy-here-it-comes expression on their faces.

"It's time . . ." I said. The eyes widened, the fingers tightened on the table edge.

". . . to set Yammer free."

"NO."

"NO."

"NO NO NO NO." The third voice in the round came in. "Don't let him go."

"He'll stay around," I said. "It will be lovely to have Yammer in our woods, flying, calling to us at night and coming to the window for a mouse or two."

"NO NO NO NO NO NO."

"Maybe he'll even have owlets and bring them to us."

Silence, as they thought about that.

"I'm going to feed him on the windowsill of my bedroom for a few days," I said. "When he knows he can always get food there, I'll open the window and he'll fly off. I'll whistle and he'll come back."

"NO, NO," said Twig. "He won't."

"Yes, he will," I said. "Don't you remember Bubo, Twig?"

"No," she said. "I was just born when we had Bubo."

"Bubo was a great horned owl," I explained. "She lived with us for four years at Vassar College, and then we let her go."

"Don't let Yammer go," said Twig.

"Bubo came back every evening to be fed," I went on. "When she found a male great horned owl in the nearby woodsy graveyard, she moved off the campus and into the woods with him. They raised two owlets in an old crow's nest."

"NO, NO," shouted Luke and Craig.

"Don't let Yammer go," said Twig.

A week later we met in the bedroom.

"Yammer has been eating mice and chicken on the windowsill for a long time now," I said. "The moment has come to open the window." They looked at me as if I were an owl executioner.

"He'll be back. He's very hungry."

Eyes widened in disbelief. No one spoke.

"He'll fly to the basswood tree to get his bearings," I said quickly. "Then I'll whistle the 'come get the food' call and he'll be right back."

"No, don't," said Twig.

"We'll feed him just a little bit tonight," I continued. "He'll still be hungry tomorrow, and he'll come back for more. We'll do this every night until he can hunt on his own."

I was facing an audience of skeptics. I had to convince them. "When I was a kid," I hastened to say, "we had a barn owl named Windy.

"He was Uncle John and Uncle Frank's lovable owl. They set him free, and he came to the sleeping porch every night to be fed. Yammer will too."

"Yammer's not a barn owl," said Craig.

That evening we let Yammer go. Twig was hopeful—she trusted that Yammer would come back. Craig was still skeptical. But Luke was brightened by a new awareness rising in him—freedom. The owl would go free. He liked that.

As we opened the window, Yammer blinked his golden eyes and swung his head in a wide circle. He saw the basswood tree, Mr. Ross's spruces, the sky, and the rising moon. Spreading his wings, he floated into the twilight.

We never saw him again.

CHAPTER 3

A Bathtub Full
of Ducklings

One spring Craig came home with six ducklings. A neighbor had found them running across his lawn and, having learned from his son that Craig George's family kept owls and lizards and the like, he turned them over to him.

They were exquisite balls of gold-and-brown down, round heads, yellow beaks, and large black eyes that twinkled. We said "Aw" when we first laid eyes on them. A baby wood duck eclipses all other "cute" animals.

We put them in a box with oats and grits and a pan of water. They peeped, rested, ran in circles, jumped, but would not eat.

After six hours of this, we called a man in Boiling Springs, Pennsylvania, who raised exotic ducks for estates and wild-fowl farms. How could we feed these tiny hatchlings that were not much bigger than golf balls?

"Put them in the bathtub with water no deeper than an inch and a half. They have to be able to reach the bottom with their beaks," he said. "Then scatter baby chick mash—you can get it at a feed store—and let it sink. Float a piece of wood so they can climb out on it and rest."

It worked. The pretty ducklings paddled around the tub feeding along the bottom and climbed up on the board. But they also jumped in the air—and that bothered us.

A duckling would look up, see the top of the tub, and pop straight up, beating its tiny wings and trying to run up the side, only to fall back down. Another would pop up. Then another and two more. The bathtub looked like a popcorn pot.

"Let them go. Let them go," cried Luke. "They want their mom."

It was Sunday, and although we had to plow the garden and prepare the ground for the flowers and vegetables, watching our new family was irresistible. We mostly hung at the tub side watching the parade.

The ducklings dove, ate, and came up fluffy and dry headed. Then, without seeming to paddle their feet, they sailed forward, backward, and in

circles like toy boats. But they kept on popping up in the air.

"Why are they doing that?" Twig asked.

"It must be related to their nest," I said, guessing wildly. "They live way up high in hollow trees."

"How do they get down? They can't fly," Craig asked.

"They fall," I said. "They can fall forty feet without even getting hurt."

The ducklings jumped and jumped.

"They must think they're still in the hollow when they see the walls of the tub," Twig said.

"Maybe," I said, "jumping for them is like paddling for the baby sea turtles I saw in Bimini. They just kept paddling even though they were in an aquarium. When they had paddled long enough to get where they ought to be, they stopped."

"I wish they would stop," said Luke.

Craig looked at me. "How do we take a bath?"

"That's going to be a problem," I replied.

"We take turns," Twig said. "I'll put the ducklings in the sink and we'll watch TV while Craig and Luke take a bath. When they're done, Yammer and I'll shower."

"Why don't we bathe with the duckies?" Luke said, and started to undress.

"No," I said. "That won't work. You'll be washing with chick mash."

But how were we going to manage the bath schedule? When we had the baby painted turtle in the tub for a couple of weeks before releasing him, it was simple enough to pick him up and put him in the sink while we showered. The ducklings would pop right out of the sink.

"We won't take baths," said Craig.

And that's how we solved it. We all went off to bed dirty. We closed the door to Twig's room, where Yammer slept, so he would not come into the bathroom and find the ducklings. If he would strike a cowboy on a horse, he would certainly strike a popping wood duckling.

The next day Twig and Luke came running to the sunporch, where I worked and kept my typewriter, library, plants, bugs, and other things pertinent to raising children and writing nature books.

"They're still jumping," Twig said. "It's sad."

"Let's take the baby ducks back to their mom," Luke said. "There are ducks on the Melvins' pond."

"Probably the wrong ones," I said. "Keep the bathroom door closed, and we'll raise them until they can live on their own."

Again we went to bed without baths, and the children did not ask for a story. They wanted to talk.

Luke: "Where does the man live who found them, Craig?"

Craig: "At the top of our mountain."

Twig: "Where did he say they were going?"

Craig: "Downhill."

Twig: "To the pond?"

Silence on Craig's part, then: "I guess so. But I don't know."

Luke: "Their mom's at the pond. I'm going to find her."

Twig: "Go to sleep. Yammer's tired."

In about a week the ducklings stopped jumping. They had, indeed, outgrown their get-out-of-the-tree-hollow behavior.

Meanwhile, the children bathed under the hose and I showered at our neighborhood swimming pool.

Luke was still looking for the mother wood duck. He and his buddy Eric Kuhn went down to the swamp pond and the stream and searched for her.

They reported a male and female mallard duck on the Town Duck Pond a quarter of a mile down the road. But mallards weren't the right kind of duck and wouldn't do.

And then came a crisis. The ducklings stopped eating. We called our family friend, Fran Uhler, the waterfowl expert at the U.S. Fish and Wildlife Service. What should we do?

"Baby wood ducks," he said, "are almost impossible to raise. If you can't find the natural mother, try putting them behind a mother mallard with a batch of young. She might let them join her brood."

We gathered the now-quiet babies in the box and drove to Teatown Lake Reservation. At the weedy end of the lake a female mallard sculled along. Three youngsters followed her through the water lilies. We sat perfectly still on the bank. Slowly they made their way toward us. The mother was calling to keep them within earshot.

We opened the box.

The wood ducklings ran out, stopped, and huddled together as they looked around. One sped toward the water. Did he hear the mother mallard calling? We will never know. All we know is that the wood ducklings set sail on the water and vanished among the emerging water plants.

We waited an hour, but they did not show themselves, nor did the mother mallard and her brood.

That night Luke said, "Let's never take wild things home again."

"Why?" I asked.

"I miss the little ducklings a lot," he said softly.

"We still have Yammer."

"Yammer likes Twig. The duckies liked me."

"That's the trouble with having pets," I said. "It's sad when they leave or die. Okay, Luke, we won't get any more wild pets, ever."

As I kissed him good night, I kicked a bucket stowed under his bed.

"What's the bucket doing here?" I asked.

"It's a home," he said.

"A home?"

"A home for salamanders."

"Lukie," I said as I pulled out the bucket and looked down on mud and moss and rocks, "I thought . . . " But I said no more.

A glistening salamander was resting on a stone, its primitive eyes looking straight ahead. "How many?"

"Five," he answered.

CHAPTER 4

The Goose and the Duck Who Were Arrested for Disturbing the Peace

One summer we moved to Poughkeepsie to our friends' house while they were away. It was not far from the Vassar College campus, where my husband, John George, taught environmental conservation. Luke had not been born yet. At that time we had a weasel, three crows, one toad, and three salamanders. The crows were named New York, Bituminous, and Light Foot. Later we acquired one Canada goose and one mallard duckling.

Bituminous departed before we moved into the house. On moving day, Light Foot got as far as the house. When we drove up the driveway and opened the door to let him out, he gave one loud rebel call. Over the trees came five crows. They swooped low, cawed a garrulous "this is it," and went off with the captive. Apparently he had been keeping in touch with his parents and siblings all the time he was with us.

"I'll be darned," said a friend who was helping us move. "They raided the corral and took back their pony."

"Now I understand why Light Foot wouldn't become a pet," I said. "His family was out there all the time plotting his escape with him."

New York had no such desires. Craig had found him when he was still half naked, and after a few meals of hamburgers and cheese he forgot what his parents looked like and became a George. When we let him out of the car, he settled into the white pine tree, watched us unpack, and arrived on the porch when everyone came in for dinner.

Twig returned the toad to the garden before we moved. She had brought him home in late spring and let him go in the house. He had hopped under the china closet. I put off getting down on my stomach to catch him, and that night he became my ecological vacuum cleaner.

As I went to get the broom to sweep up the crumbs the kids spilled on the floor, I noticed that the ants were coming out of the old floorboards. Twig and I paused to watch them carry off the food. Out from under the china closet hopped the toad. He snatched some of them up with his long tongue and retreated. Soon there were no crumbs and no ants. This beat sweeping and vacuuming by a long shot, so the toad stayed until we moved.

The Canada goose came to us one May morning when a friend, Bill, came by with a goose egg. The gosling's egg tooth had cut a round circle at the top of the egg, and the little thing was struggling within.

"Where did you get it?" we asked.

"In a nest," Bill said. "The mother goose had led the hatched goslings off to the water. This egg was left behind."

Before he had finished his story, the small wet head of the gosling poked out of the shell. She struggled, broke free, and lay still.

"It's mine," cried Twig, jumping in excitement.

"Ours," said Craig.

We carried the tiny thing inside and put it in a box under an electric light bulb to dry. In about an hour she was fluffy, big eyed, and so cute she turned on the mothering instincts in all of us. She was bound to survive. We put down chick mash and she ate. Unlike many birds that are naked and blind when they hatch, geese and ducks, which are precocial birds, can walk and eat shortly after hatching. They also are very susceptible to imprinting. That is, they think anyone who feeds them upon hatching is their mother and that they look like him, her, or it, be that a person, bird, beast, or cardboard feeding tray pulled across the lawn. Mom is what moves and feeds you.

Twig learned that if she fed the gosling from her hand, she would be a mother goose. She stuck with it a few days, but soon it fell upon me to feed the goose most of the time. I became Mother Goose. When I sat down, the goose sat down. When I went into the kitchen, the goose went into the kitchen. When I hung the clothes outdoors on the clothesline, the goose stretched up her neck as if to hang the clothes too.

Then Bill came by with another egg that was about to hatch. Out of this shell wobbled a mallard duckling.

Duck dropped his head on my thumb and shivered. Craig put him under his shirt and warmed him against his bare stomach. When he was dry, we put him under the electric light bulb until he seemed strong, then placed him at the pan of chick mash. He did not eat. When after three hours he still had not eaten, we made a wet pablum of the mash and fed it to him in an eyedropper. Duck perked up, and by the end of the day we put him down at the pan where Goose was eating. He watched her, learned, and ate.

Presently we had a goose that thought she was a person, and a duck that thought he was a goose.

When I went to the kitchen, the goose went to the kitchen and the duck went to the kitchen. When I sat down at the table, the goose flew up to the seat beside me and sat down and the duck flew up beside her and sat down. When I went out on the porch, the goose went out on the porch and the duck went out on the porch. Then we all sat down on the steps—first me, then the goose, then the duck.

We were quite a spectacle, and people began to talk about us. They said our family played tag and hopscotch with a goose and a duck. It was true. They said when we drove the car, Twig, Craig, and Luke sat in the back of the station wagon and the goose and the duck sat in the "power seat." It was true. And they said on hot days we all got under the hose with a goose and a duck, and that was true too.

They also said that we put the goose and duck in the doghouse at night and closed them in with a bread board. This was also true, but it was not unkind as the statement implied. We were protecting them from Nipper, our pet weasel, who occasionally got out at night. He was the only pet that we had to keep in a pen. He was a charming pup, but an obstreperous teenager.

Nipper came by his name honestly. At feeding time he nipped any toe, ankle, or heel he could find. Feeding him was pure theater. Neighborhood kids, and their parents, would gather in our yard to watch. First Goose and Duck were closed into the doghouse, the dog and cat were put in the car, and the children and adults dispatched to the roof of the car or up the ropes of the swing. When all was ready, one of us would walk up to Nipper's box and lift the door. Out of the door like a meteor streaked Nipper. He circled the lawn sniffing for food, leaped over sandbox, toy trucks, bikes, and

hoses, and would have settled for a heel or two if anyone had remained on the ground. Sitting on stumps and on swings, we waited for him to wear himself out.

When at last he was merely running, not jetting around, we would put down his ground steak laced with vitamins and fish oil and jump back up to safety. Instantly he would smell food, wheel, and like a rippling whip cross the yard to the plate. He devoured the food the way fire devours gasoline, and then the real show began. We had to get him back in his box. Since he chased anything that ran, I would take off at a trot, and Nipper would follow. The object was to stay just far enough ahead of him to keep him interested in biting me, but not let him get me. At the last minute I would head for his box and jump over it. Nipper would follow me and jump into the box. The door would be dropped, and the show was over. Seconds later Nipper would be asleep. Weasels sleep as hard as they play. We could even pick him up and pet him when he was in the deep sleep of the well-exercised and well-fed weasel.

Once Nipper was in his box, we could let Goose and Duck out of the doghouse. They usually wandered onto the grassy lawn and began eating. Geese are grazers, but mallard ducks are not.

They are dabblers. But Duck's mother ate grass, so Duck ate it too. He would snap off the greenery, pass it through his beak, and spit it out the other side. A goose for a mother or not, he could not go against his inherited dislike of grass.

One night we forgot to put the board against the doghouse door. Goose and Duck awoke when the moonlight streamed in upon them, and they got up. Goose stepped out of the house to find her mother. I was nowhere to be found, and so she started down College Avenue, calling. Duck was right behind her, quacking.

A policeman happened to come by on his midnight rounds. He saw the pair, pulled over to the curb, and opened his door to make sure he was sane. Goose, upon seeing what appeared to be her mother, flew into the car and sat down in the power seat. Duck flew after his mother and sat down beside her.

The policeman scratched his head and thought about Thanksgiving. He closed the door and drove to the precinct. He arrested them for "disturbing the peace."

The children who lived nearby awoke the next morning to see Goose and Duck in the yard of the police station and came running down College Avenue and knocked on our door.

"Mrs. George," little Mary Ann said breathlessly,

"your goose and duck are at the police station. Sergeant Meyers has them."

"They've been arrested," said her brother. "The policeman said he was going to eat them."

"Come on, let's get them," his sister said, and ran to our station wagon.

We arrived at the police station a few minutes later and found Sergeant Meyers hosing down his squad car. Goose and Duck were splashing and flapping in the spray.

"Sir," I said, "thanks for finding our pets. I've come to take them home."

"What makes you think they're yours?" he

asked. "They look like a wild Canada goose and a wild mallard duck to me."

Of course, he was right. They were wild birds.

"We raised them," I said. "They think we're their parents. They follow us everywhere we go."

"They follow me everywhere I go." He walked up the steps and into the office. The goose walked up the steps into the office, and the duck walked up the steps following the goose. Twig, Craig, and I walked up the steps following the goose and the duck.

"How are we going to prove they are ours?" Twig asked nervously.

"We'll just be ourselves," I said.

We sat down on the bench across from the sergeant's desk. Goose flew up and sat down beside me, and Duck flew up and sat down beside Goose.

"See?" we said to Sergeant Meyers. "They're ours."

"So what?" the sergeant said. "They sit down beside me, too."

I walked over to the desk and leaned on it. The goose flew onto the desk. The duck flew onto the desk, the papers flew through the air, and the goose sat down and the duck sat down and honked and quacked.

"Okay, okay, lady," said the policeman, grabbing the papers. "They're yours. They're yours."

And so we put Goose and Duck in the station wagon and drove home.

At the end of the summer we moved back to the campus. We couldn't take Goose and Duck with us, so I called the principal of a private school with a pond and asked if the odd pair could live there. He was delighted to have them.

Goose and Duck quickly adapted to their new parents. They followed the schoolchildren around the playgrounds, visited their classrooms, and swam behind the canoes.

One day a group of migrating mallards came to the school pond, and Duck took one look at them and abandoned his mother. With his own kind he discovered food at the bottom of the pond and found it far superior to grass. He took up with the bottom eaters.

In the morning, when the mallard ducks migrated on south, Duck went with them.

Goose stayed at the school. Ganders came and courted her, but she paid them no heed. She was imprinted on people, and in her mind a gander was not a proper mate. She stayed at the school for many years. Then she disappeared.

CHAPTER 5

A Trouble-Making Crow

The year Luke was one year old, we moved to Chappaqua, New York, and bought our first house. The house sits on a wooded hillside. Through the leafless trees in winter we see the neighbors. In summer we seem to be alone. Uphill from the house there is a spring where salamanders and frogs dwell. The hill is steep and makes for wild sledding in winter. Downhill is a swamp and a shallow lake with a deer woods beyond.

With us on our arrival in our new home came New York and three salamanders. New York walked in the front door and out the back and flew off to explore the neighborhood. Late in the afternoon he settled himself in hemlocks in the backyard. The next day, the first day of school, he followed us down the hill to the bus stop and sat on the rail fence.

At the bus stop were Sis Melvin and Tom and Merry, among others. This was the first day of school for Tom as well as for Craig. Merry Melvin was in her stroller, and Luke was in my backpack. Seven-year-old Twig sat on the fence with New York. Sis glanced from her to the crow. She tapped my shoulder.

"See that big black bird?" she whispered. "It just sits there on the fence. Do you suppose something's wrong with it?"

"That's New York, our pet crow," I said. "He likes people."

"I see," she answered, and the conversation stopped for several minutes.

That was the beginning of a friendship that has lasted to this day.

I went home and unpacked my typewriter and put it in the winterized sunporch at the rear of the house. It was the perfect place for me to work. The windows and glass door looked out on the backyard and woods. It was also a place where the kids could almost always find me.

Craig came running into the porch one day in late autumn.

"Mom," he said, his voice filled with horror, "New York dives at little Hilde Black's eyes. She has to hit him."

I had read just enough about crows to know what that meant. Crows are vindictive. If a person hurts a crow, it will sometimes return the pain with vengeance. Hilde must have hurt him. "Eyes," I thought—he was diving at Hilde's eyes. A chill ran down my spine.

"New York has to go," I said urgently. "Help me catch him."

"Are you going to kill him?" Craig cried.

"I may have to."

"No, Mom, no. He's a bird. He doesn't know he's bad."

"People come first," I said. "How would you feel if Hilde was blinded by our crow?"

His eyes widened as he understood the seriousness of New York's vengeance.

"I don't want to kill him," I said. "I want to

take him far away and let him go—far from Hilde."

"Will he dive at anyone else's eyes?"

"No. Hilde must have kicked him or hurt him somehow, and he's taking it out on her. He won't forget. Crows are like that."

Craig ran into the yard to find New York, and I went to the cellar for an animal carrying case.

"I've got him," I heard Craig call as I came out the door.

I walked slowly toward them, trying to act as if I had nothing more serious in mind than weeding the garden.

New York saw right through us. He gave out a frantic cry and took off for the top of the ash tree. We followed below, calling him lovingly and cheerfully. "Haw," he called, and flew into the woods to slink off along the tree limbs. We knew we would never get him by pretending to be dear old friends, so we went inside to make supper.

"Mom," Craig called, "New York's back." I knew better than to let the bird see me, but I was so worried about Hilde, I ran outside anyway. With a raucous caw, New York flew from the picnic table to the sunporch roof. He rasped out short caws of distress and pumped his head up and down. He was telling all crowdom that he knew what was going on.

That night three silent and unhappy children went to bed.

"New York has to go," I said. "We can't let him hurt Hilde."

"We know."

In the darkness of night I approached New York on his roost in the ash tree. He could not see to fly. I threw a beach towel over him and put him in the carrying case, a feat I don't care to repeat.

The next day Twig and Craig said their heart-breaking farewells to New York and then went out the door to catch the school bus. Craig paused and looked back at me.

"It's okay, Mom," he said.

"Thank you" was all I could answer.

I wiped a tear, put Luke in his car seat, and drove north on the Taconic Parkway to James Baird Park.

I opened the door of the carrier and a wild bird, not our friendly New York, took off into the woods. His eyes were hard and glistening and his feathers were pressed to his body. He would never forgive me for catching him in a towel, any more than he would forgive little Hilde for whatever she had done.

We did not feel bad about removing New York to distant woods. Dr. Kalmbach, the U.S. Department of Agriculture's crow expert, wrote in a scientific paper, "Crows are vindictive." I was shocked to read that. My father, a scientist, had taught my brothers and me not to anthropomorphize—that is, not to read human emotions and attributes into animals. They did not hate, love, envy, or even feel happy. So what was this vindictiveness, a very complex human emotion that Dr. Kalmbach was seeing in a crow?

It was this: Dr. Kalmbach kept a pet crow, the better to understand the bird that farmers were at war with for stealing corn and other crops. Next door to him lived a man who raised cabbages and showed them at the state fair. Every day he would proudly tend them with his yappy dog following at his heels.

One day amidst crow caws and dog yaps, the neighbor stormed into Dr. Kalmbach's office.

"Your crow is tearing the leaves off my prize cabbages," he said angrily. "Stop him or I'll shoot him."

To avoid trouble, Dr. Kalmbach called his crow down from the maple tree between the two yards and spanked him with a cabbage leaf.

"No cabbages, no cabbages," he snapped. He did not go so far as to think the bird knew English, but he did know that crows discipline crows and know when they have been punished. I knew what he was talking about. Once, Luke and I saw a group of crows come through the woods chasing a fellow crow. They dove at him, yelled at him, and hit him with their wings. He tumbled, fell, and escaped into the underbrush. When he didn't come out, they flew off.

Dr. Kalmbach's crow seemed to understand that he had been disciplined. He flew to a limb in the maple tree between the two yards and drooped his wings and head. For two days he sulked, but he did not tear the cabbage leaves.

On the third day Dr. Kalmbach heard the neighbor's dog yapping, and the unmistakable sound of cabbage leaves being torn asunder. He ran outside. His crow was holding a piece of meat in his feet and flying just above the nose of the little dog, who ran down one cabbage row and up the next tearing the cabbages asunder.

CHAPTER 6

A Talking Crow

Several years after Light Foot, Bituminous, and then New York came and went, Crowbar came into our lives.

Craig found him on the ground in a spruce grove. A violent windstorm had knocked bird and nest out of a tree. Craig looked around for his parents, saw none, and tucked the almost-naked nestling into his shirt and carried him home.

"His name's Crowbar," he said as he put him on the kitchen table. The little crow was somewhat younger than New York had been when we brought him home, and so we knew this bird was going to be more deeply imprinted on us. He would indeed be a member of the family.

The scrappy little crow looked at us, rolled to his back, and clawed the air as if to tear us to pieces. He screamed like an attacking warrior.

I went to the refrigerator, took out a cold

cheeseburger, and stuffed a bite in his mouth, pressing it with my finger to make sure he swallowed. He did, and instantly changed his tune. He blinked his pale-blue eyes and got to his feet. Taking a wide stance to keep from falling over, he fluttered his stubby wings. In bird talk this means, "I am a helpless baby bird—feed me." We fed him until he couldn't open his beak.

At the end of the day we had a pet crow. Crows are smart. They know a good thing when they see it.

But it was not just the food. He was young and craved our attention. He cuddled against Luke, begged until Craig petted his head and chin, and dropped spoons and forks off the kitchen table until someone talked to him. He was ours, and he let us know just what that meant.

He did concede one thing to his heredity, however: He slept in the apple tree outside the kitchen window. This greatly pleased me. Although a red fox named Fulva; two mink, Vison and Mustelid; and three skunks had trained themselves to use a litter box while in the house, Crowbar, New York, and our other crows had no inclination to do so. Fortunately they spent most of their time outside, and when they did come in, they treated the house like their nest and kept it clean.

By autumn Crowbar was Crowbar George to Twig, Craig, and Luke. He would wake them at dawn by rapping on their windows with his beak. The three would come downstairs and set the table, including a plate for Crowbar. They would scramble the eggs, serve them up, and open the window. Crowbar would fly to his plate and gulp his food like the young gluttonous crow that he was.

Then he would fly out the window to the apple tree and wait until Twig, Craig, and now Luke came out the door and down the front steps on their way to school. He would drop to the ground and walk beside them all the way down the hill to the school bus stop. Like New York he would sit on the rail fence. When the bus came, he would fly back to the kitchen window, and I would know my children were safely on their way to school. Other mothers had to go down to the bus stop and wait. I sent a crow.

Meanwhile I was reading every scientific paper about crows that I could get my hands on. I read that crows are hard to study because they're so smart. They easily elude and outwit the observer. They hide. They sneak through tree limbs. They count. A farmer learned that if he went crow hunting in the woods, he would not see a crow. They knew about guns. To foil them, the farmer took a friend into the woods with him. The farmer hid and the friend walked out across the fields and away. The crows did not make an appearance until the farmer left.

Crows, I also read, have a language. They communicate with each other. Three caws are an identification—"I'm so-and-so crow." Five desperately given caws mean there is an enemy around—a hawk, an owl, a man with a gun. Many caws given with passion and fury say, "Come—mob the owl." The crow fact that amazed me most, however, was that they can detect poisoned food and warn each other not to eat it.

They can recognize death in any form it takes. In an experiment by Dr. Kalmbach, two farmers who shot some crows in their cornfield found they could never again get close enough to the crows to shoot. Their wives could, however. When they came to the fields, the crows went right on eating within ten feet of them. The farmers decided that the crows recognized them because they wore pants. They put on skirts and aprons and went out to shoot the crows. They still could not get within gunshot range. Putting their heads together once more, they figured the crows must see the guns and know they meant death. They disguised the guns in brooms and went out to the cornfields to kill the crows. Before they got within range the crows were gone.

It must be, wrote Dr. Kalmbach, that when a man picks up a gun, he takes on an aggressive attitude that the crows read. They flee.

Appended to one report on crows was this: "Crows can learn to talk as do parrots or myna birds."

With that we began Crowbar's English lessons.

"Hello, hello, hello," we said slowly and distinctly many times over. "Hello, hello, hello." This went on for days and weeks.

He did not speak. He looked at us intently, his throat feathers rising and falling. Then he would wipe his beak, a reaction to frustration.

"I give up," I said to Twig, and had no more than gotten the words out of my mouth than John

Priori, who delivered the milk, came in the back door.

"Oh, good," he said. "You're in the kitchen. I thought I heard you up in the apple tree saying 'hello.' "

"It's Crowbar," we shouted. "Crowbar is talking." Twig and I ran outside to listen.

"Hello," said the clever bird. "Hello, hello, hello."

"Crowbar," Twig said slowly and thoughtfully, "is really the smartest person on the block."

Crowbar did not rest on his laurels. He soon figured out how to make use of that word.

The neighbors on our wooded hillside come outside in summer to picnic and cook on their grills. Most have moved to the suburbs from New York City and know little about the country, much less its wild membership. Crowbar discovered that if he alit on a food-laden table and said, "Hello," he terrified these people. A large black bird might be tolerated, but one that spoke English was too much. They ran into their houses and closed their doors. Crowbar then helped himself to the hamburgers, strawberry shortcake, cheese, and nuts. When he was stuffed, he flew back to his apple tree.

Twig and I were walking under his tree one day as he was returning from one of these picnics. He alit, cocked his eye, and said, "Hiya, Babe."

Because Crowbar was completely free, our new neighbors had no idea he was a pet. Soon the police began to get complaints about a bird that took the clothespins out of their laundry and dumped clean shirts and towels on the ground.

The officers would arrive and, finding only an ordinary crow sitting on a fence or flying off through the trees, they would peg the complainers as cranks and depart. The complaints persisted, however, and one policeman, a hunter and wise to the ways of crows, brought a BB gun to the scene.

As the officer rounded the house, gun in hand, Crowbar gave five frantic caws. Birds stopped singing; crows disappeared. The policeman stood in a silent world where nothing moved but a breeze-touched shirt that Crowbar had not yet released to the ground.

"That bird won't be back," he said to the complainer. "Crows see a gun and they're off—for good."

He left, smiling at his own cleverness. When the patrol car was out of sight, Crowbar dropped down to the wash line and dropped the breeze-touched shirt to the ground.

So much for knowing it all.

CHAPTER 7

The Mystery of the Pond in the Foyer

Our menagerie increased rapidly after a neighbor, Sean Sears, who had a passion for cement, built a pool of slate and cement in the foyer of the house. We needed an indoor pond where we could keep the creatures of our streams and lakes and come to know them.

Luke was almost a year old when we moved into the brown shingled house. By the time we had an indoor pond, he was six and a full-fledged gatherer; and, sadly for all of us, John and I divorced at this time. Twig, Craig, and Luke would stay with me in the house we had come to love, and they would see their father as often as possible. I think we all lived through the difficulty of this period with the help of each other and our friends, wild and civilized.

When the pond was finished, we found ourselves caught up in the wacky wonderfulness of the inhabitants. Not only did they give us something to think about other than what would happen to us as a single-parent family, but they led us into an engrossing mystery.

We rimmed the pond with ferns and filled it with water. Then Luke set out for the swamp and stream with seines, buckets, and his buddy Eric Kuhn. Within the month they put seven sunfish, six crayfish, two large-mouth bass, one baby painted turtle, and five bullfrog tadpoles in the pond in the foyer.

"All brown creatures," Twig said of their catch, and spent her next allowance on three goldfish.

In September the bullfrog tadpoles disappeared.

"Someone ate them," said Craig.

"Crowbar," said Luke. "I saw him walking around the edge of the pond."

"Maybe they changed into frogs and hopped away," said Twig.

Twig searched the downstairs for young bullfrogs, then reported back to her brothers. "They're not in the house. Besides, they would die out of the water and we'd smell them by now."

We gathered in the kitchen for some quick energy for thought—milk and cookies.

"Someone ate them," Luke said, and eyed Crowbar, who had arrived on the windowsill. He had heard us in the kitchen and knew this usually meant food. He hopped to the sink and picked up a silver spoon. He was sneaking toward the window with the spoon when Luke jumped up and intercepted him.

"That's Mom's," he said, taking the spoon. "You did it, Crowbar. You steal. See, Craig?"

"He likes pretty things," said Craig defensively. "Tadpoles are not pretty."

"Their moms think they are," said Luke.

Several weeks went by before the next mysterious event took place. Two of the seven sunfish disappeared. We gathered around the pond.

"They're dead," Craig said. "I see them on the bottom." Twig looked, saw the dead sunfish, and went to the basement for the fish net. After a skirmish she caught her goldfish and put them in a bowl in her room.

"I don't want them killed," she said.

"Crowbar did it," persisted Luke.

"Crowbar gets so much to eat, he doesn't have to fish," I said, and glanced at the dining-room table. It was Luke's birthday, and we had placed paper cups filled with nuts beside the seven paper plates.

"Speaking of Crowbar," I said, "we'd better cover those nuts, or our good friend will eat them." I went to the kitchen for mugs.

The kitchen window was always slightly ajar for Crowbar. He could come and go at his pleasure. We carried the mugs into the dining room and placed them over the paper cups of nuts. Between trips we kept the swinging door closed, so that Crowbar wouldn't get any ideas.

But Crowbar already had ideas. People see the world from an earthbound level. But ah, the bird. From the top of the roof, trees, and telephone poles, Crowbar got a bird's-eye view of the world. He saw the entire neighborhood as well as what went on inside our house. From the trees he peered down at us through the windows.

When we had covered all the nuts, Crowbar hopped to the floor and walked through the foyer door to join his siblings.

"Hi, Crowbar," Luke said. "Did you eat the tadpoles?"

"You'd better put Crowbar outside," I said. "Luke's friends will be coming soon, and some of the parents are not going to like a crow in the house."

Craig put his hand to the floor, Crowbar climbed to his shoulder, and they went outside together. I went back to the kitchen and mixed the icing for the birthday cake.

Soon I heard that unmistakable sound of a crow gulping food, and I swung open the door to the dining room. Crowbar was on the floor devouring nuts. Strangely enough, all the mugs on the table were in place.

The icing and guests notwithstanding, I had to find out how he had gotten those nuts. I shooed him away and picked up the nuts. He ruffled his feathers and strutted into the sunporch. I went back to the kitchen, closing the door behind me. After a few minutes I opened the door a crack and peered into the dining room.

Crowbar was on the table. He took a mug handle in his beak and shoved the mug over the edge of the table. The paper cup and nuts fell out from under it. He pulled the mug back where he had found it, poked it once with his beak to arrange it correctly, flew to the floor, and ate.

"Crowbar," I said, coming into the room, "you are too darned smart."

I scolded him as I gathered him up in his taffeta wings and threw him out the door. He glided to the oak tree, turned his back on the house, and sulked. Crows do not like to be scolded. I had the awful feeling that he was plotting revenge. New York had already taught us what that could mean.

A few minutes later Barney the hound dog, who lived at the bottom of the hill with the Hart family, came up the road. He was escorting one of the partygoers. When they entered the yard, Crowbar dropped down from the apple tree and skimmed just over Barney's nose. The hound snapped at him, missed, and gave chase. Try as Barney would, and he desperately tried, he could not catch the bird. This was Crowbar's favorite sport, and in view of the scolding he had just received, I was sure he was paying me back. Chaos erupted as little boys raced around the house behind Crowbar and Barney, cheering and laughing. Twig and I shouted, "Cake!" above the din and the young guests straggled indoors. Barney collapsed on the ground and Crowbar swept into his apple tree.

"Hello, hello, hello. Hiya, Babe," he called.

When the cake was consumed and the presents opened, the kids hurried outside. Barney jumped up to meet them. Crowbar flew just out of reach of his jaws. Around and around the house they went; around and around went the laughing boys.

"Craig," I finally said as the parade came past the kitchen window for the third time, "get your crow before someone calls the ASPCA and fines Crowbar for cruelty to dogs."

Craig lured Crowbar into the kitchen with cake and cheese and closed the doors and the window. Barney went home.

"Best party yet," said a grimy boy as he started out the door to meet his parents. "Can I come back tomorrow?"

Through all the Crowbar diversions death went on in the pool. Scales, a small bass, rolled over and died. His belly was striped with bloody streaks, so I phoned the conservation officer and asked if the native bass were suffering from any disease that brought blood to the surface of their bodies. He knew of none.

One morning as Luke was coming downstairs he saw the other bass, called Bass, who had tripled his size, open his mouth and swallow a sunfish.

"Bass is the villain," Luke said as he came in to breakfast. "I saw him eat a sunfish."

"Pretty soon we'll have just Bass and nothing else," said Craig.

"We've got four sunfish, four crayfish, one large-mouth bass, and one painted turtle," Luke said with the organization of a fledgling scientist. "I'll bet Bass ate all the others; the tadpoles too."

Life in the pool, we could see, was going to narrow down to one survivor. I, like Luke, bet on Bass. He and his kind are the lions of the freshwater world. They eat just about anything. A friend who fished on Byram Lake in the next township pulled up twenty- and thirty-pound bass using mice as bait. Most had been swallowed whole.

Twig bet on Crowbar. She too had seen him standing on the edge of the pool looking in. Craig thought the problem was lack of oxygen. So he tested the water and discovered that was not the problem.

Then Bass rolled over and died. He had the same bloody belly that the first bass did. We were all wrong, and we stopped guessing.

Later that month Twig asked if she could take two of the crayfish to science class. They were studying invertebrates.

"Now we have four sunfish, two crayfish, and one painted turtle," Luke said, hanging over the pond. "Bass is gone and everybody should be fine."

But they weren't. Another sunfish died.

"Three sunfish, two crayfish, and one painted turtle," Luke said.

We eliminated the painted turtle as the villain. He never ate anything but ant eggs from the pet shop, but to make sure we returned him to the swamp at the bottom of the hill.

Another sunfish died and the last one was tilting like a sinking ship. Luke got down on his knees.

"It's the crayfish," he said. "The crayfish are the villains. They reach up and scratch the fish on their bellies until they bleed to death. Then they eat them."

"Ugh," said Twig. "How horrible."

"Crayfish have to live," said Luke.

After that lesson we decided we would not mix species in such a confined area. We would keep only one species in the pond. The noble large-mouth bass was our choice.

Bass the Second became a family pet. We could lift him out of the water to have his picture taken and to measure him. He grew to be twenty-four inches.

Then disaster struck Bass the Second. The electricity went out on the entire eastern seaboard one night, and the pump that jetted air into the water went dead. Bass gasped for oxygen.

After a wet scramble by flashlight, we caught

our friend and put him in a bucket of water. Craig and Luke ran all the way down to the Harts' pond in the dark and let him go.

Several months later, avid fisherman and neighbor Ernie Dickinson caught Bass the Third for us. Unfortunately, Bass the Third met the same fate as Bass the Second when we had another power failure. The kids were all in college when this happened, so I settled for goldfish.

I still have them. They can live in stale water. Even crayfish can't do that, so maybe goldfish are at the top of the water pyramid.

CHAPTER 8

Raising a Raccoon

No sooner had we solved the mystery of the foyer pond than Craig came home with a baby raccoon.

After a late spring deluge a baby raccoon came swimming out of the culvert under the road at the bottom of the hill and into Craig's hands. He was shivering so hard, he couldn't cry. Craig brought the sopping kit to the sunporch. I dropped what I was doing to look for a baby doll's bottle while Craig dried the little fellow under his shirt against his bare stomach. We mixed raccoon pup formula of condensed milk, water, vitamins, and honey. When he stopped shivering, I held him against me and stuck the bottle in his wide mouth. He lapped then, sucking so hard the milk ran down his belly and me. We named the little guy Hands.

For the next week or so we took turns feeding the scraggly, noisy 'coon child. At the sound of his ratchety cry one or another of us would warm formula and bottle, wrap him in a towel, and sit down in the rocking chair to feed him. He would clutch the bottle with his feet and knead it as if it were his mother. As the milk flowed into his cupped mouth, the abrasive hunger call became a contented purr.

Like the goose and the duck, Hands became imprinted on his nurturers and was soon a member of the family. To make the adjustment he changed from a night creature to a day creature, used the litter box, and purred when we scratched his head and ears.

When he was big enough to eat on his own, Craig and Luke brought an old barrel out of the basement and put it in a crotch of the apple tree by the sunporch door. This was the raccoon baby's home.

In the morning he would lean out of the barrel and wait for one of us to pick him up and put him on the ground. He was still too young to make it down the tree by himself. I had learned this from a pet raccoon, Lotor, who had given birth to two babies.

When they were about the age of Hands, the little raccoons could climb up trees, but they couldn't climb down. One day they scampered joyfully up a tree, ears back, eyes shining. It was fun.

Ten or twelve feet above the ground they tried to turn around and come down headfirst, as raccoons do. They could not. A great ratcheting cry went up.

Lotor loped up the tree, grabbed one by the scruff of its neck, and dropped it to the ground with a thud. Then she dropped the other one, hurried down the tree, and stood over them while she scolded them with snarls. I was astonished. I had always believed that wild animals did not have to discipline their young. Not so, as these youngsters were constantly trying Lotor's patience, climbing trees, running away, fighting. Every day they got some comeuppance from their mother.

Little Hands did not get himself into such situations. He stayed right at our heels all day.

Although crows and raccoons don't interact in the wild, Crowbar and Hands developed a symbiotic relationship. That is, they were mutually helpful to each other.

It worked like this: Crowbar learned to open the bread box and help himself. Hands knew this meant food and would stand under him. Pieces of bread would drop to the floor, either because Crowbar was a messy eater or because he wanted to share—we never knew which. Luke was of the mind that Crowbar was sloppy. Craig thought he was kind.

Hands for his part would satisfy Crowbar's love for shiny objects. He was a fingerer. He opened drawers and found wonderful objects like earrings, paper clips, old keys, and measuring spoons. He would pick them up and carry them to the floor or outdoors to explore them with his handlike paws. When he found them inedible, he would leave them scattered wherever he dropped them.

With crow delight—*caw! dong!*—Crowbar would swoop down, pick them up, and hide them in his apple tree.

The two often went to the lake at the bottom of the hill to fish with Luke. Hands rode on Luke's shoulders. Crowbar followed overhead. He knew the combination of Luke and Hands meant fish. He waited in the trees above them. When Luke caught a fish, he would toss it on the ground for Hands. Hands would roll it in his paws until it was shredded, then begin to eat. Crowbar alit on the ground, and Hands let him steal a share of the feast.

One day, while the two were eating, Barney appeared. Crowbar got on his wings and sailed over Barney's nose. The hound leaped, snapped, missed, and the chase was on. When Barney finally lay down to catch his breath, the fish was eaten. Crowbar didn't seem to care. Leading Barney in a chase was far sweeter than fish, and besides, there was always food at the kitchen window.

CHAPTER 9

Crowbar Goes to the Bank

The sandbox was Crowbar's favorite spot. When Twig and Craig played in the sandbox with Luke, they dumped into the sand a bucket of glittering spoons, bottle caps, toy soldiers, coffee cans and lids. At the sight of the sparkle, Crowbar would materialize from the trees and join them. He walked around forts and castles, picking up bright treasures and carrying them to the apple tree.

One day as I was working at my desk, Twig came to the door of the sunporch, her hands on her hips.

"I'm not going to play with that crow anymore," she said. "He takes all my toys."

I smiled. Here was my Twig. She was seeing the human in Crowbar. But she did have a point, after all. It must be maddening when you are counting on shaping a castle turret with a spoon and a crow steals it.

"Why don't you slide down the slide?" I suggested. "Crows can't slide down slides. Their feet have pads that hold them fast to perches."

She went back to her brothers, and the next time I looked up the three were sliding down the slide.

Then down from the roof sailed Crowbar. He swept his black wings upward, then down, and alit on the top of the slide. We all stared. Would he slide? He stepped on the steeply slanted board—and was stuck.

Twig waved to me; I waved back to her. We had outwitted a crow, which we both knew was a very hard thing to do.

No sooner had we gone on with our businesses than Crowbar flew to the sandbox. He picked up a coffee-can lid, carried it to the top of the slide, stepped on it, and—*zoom*—we had a sliding crow.

Crowbar was indeed a character. In the morning when the children were in school, he would sit beside my foot when I was working at my typewriter and brood over it. He would lift his feathers and lean against my ankle as if it were some cherished object. Sometimes he would go into a trance and fall over.

Unaware that I was being used, I would pick

him up and pet him. He would make soft noises, then hop to my desk and fly off with a paper clip. I would laugh, knowing I had been had—but I never learned. He repeated this game many times, and I always fell for it.

When school reopened after spring vacation, Crowbar began to disappear every day at noon. He would walk to the open door, fly to the ash tree, and sneak uphill into the woods.

For hours I would neither see nor hear him. I assumed he was resting quietly in some leafy tree, which birds do for longer periods than most people realize.

One day a little neighbor girl, Sally, came to my door.

"Mrs. George," she said, "I think Crowbar has enough money to buy a sports car."

"What do you mean?" I asked.

"He comes down to the middle school every day for lunch," she said. "We feed him sandwiches and throw him our milk money. He picks up the money and flies off with it. He must be very rich."

"The middle school," I said, and remembered the crow's-eye view of the ecosystem. Of course: While soaring above the trees, he had spotted the kids and their food and shiny money. I wondered what else Crowbar knew about our town. He probably knew about the baseball games and picnics, the people getting on and off the trains, and the town Dumpsters. But apparently most fascinating to him were the kids at the middle school eating sandwiches and flipping shiny coins into the air, and so it was to them he went at noon.

"We can't find where he hides his money," Sally went on. "Could you help us?"

"I'll try," I answered dubiously, "but crows are clever. He may be investing it in Wall Street."

She didn't laugh, so I answered more seriously. "I'll meet you on the playground tomorrow at noon, and we'll see what he's up to."

Crowbar was walking among the children

when I arrived. Sally saw me and came running. Crowbar, who undoubtedly knew I was there, ignored me. A boy waved a coin and spun it in the air. When it sparkled to the ground, Crowbar hopped upon it and took it in his beak.

When he had a beakful of money, he skimmed low over the grass and laboriously climbed into a sugar maple tree that edged the playground. He looked as if he had stolen the crown jewels.

"See?" Sally said. "He hides his money, but we don't know where. He won't hide it while we're watching."

"He sure won't," I said. "Crows are very secretive. Other birds' nests are easy to find by following the parents when they are carrying food home to the young. But not crows.

"They won't go near their nests while you're watching. Those bright coins are kind of like Crowbar's nest. He doesn't want you to find them."

"Seems so," said Sally. "He waits till the bell rings and we have to go inside; then he flies away and we can't see where he goes."

The bell rang, Sally dashed off, and I sat down to see if I could outwait my friend. I could not. After half an hour I gave up and went home.

About a week later I came out of the bank, which is next to the middle school, and saw

Crowbar flying low over the recreation field, laboriously carrying his load of quarters and dimes. I stepped back into the doorway. He flew over the fence and the parked cars, then swept up to the rainspout of the bank. He looked around and then deposited his money in the bank's rainspout.

There is something uncanny about crows.

New York gave me my first experience with this otherworldly attribute.

One afternoon the director of the Bronx Zoo and his wife, who were friends of my aunt and uncle, came to visit. Mrs. Tee Van was a very accomplished nature artist, and I was flattered that she would come calling. The day before, I had returned from a speaking engagement and had brought home to Twig the hotel shampoo, soap, and shoe-shine rag. She had put the shoe-shine rag in the dollhouse that stood on the porch.

We adults sat down in the living room to get acquainted. The children and New York played on the porch in view of us. At one point in the conversation Mrs. Tee Van looked out the window and saw New York walking on the porch railing. She smiled when she saw him.

"I had a pet crow when I was young," she said, and walked to the window. "I adored him. He was so clever." She paused. "Your crow's legs are so shiny. How do you manage that?"

Hardly had she spoken than New York flew to the dollhouse, picked up the shoe-shine cloth, and walked with it in his beak slowly along the porch railing.

Dr. Tee Van and I chuckled, but Mrs. Tee Van did not. She turned to me, visibly upset by what seemed to be a crow answering her question.

"We must go," she said. "That's just too uncanny."

"A funny coincidence," I said, forcing myself to laugh.

"No," she answered. "Crows are eerie. We have a lot to learn."

CHAPTER 10

The Demise of the Kestrel

During the summer of Hands and Crowbar we acquired Iliad the kestrel. He was a gift from my brothers, who were two of the first falconers in the United States. My brother John's daughter, Karen, came east for a visit and brought the beautiful little falcon with her. This was before the laws governing birds of prey were passed.

As Iliad sat on my finger, feeling more like a breath of wind than a bird, I thought back on my thirteenth birthday, when John and Frank had given me another kestrel. I named him Bad Boy after he bit me and sank his sharp talons into my hand.

I had five wonderful years with that bird. I watched him speed through the sky like a crossbow, climb on the spiraling thermals until he was out of sight, then dive toward me at bullet speed. Just above my upstretched hand he would break his fall with a sweep of his wings and land on my fist as softly as thistledown. He and I explored the fields and meadows by day, and at night he would sit on my shoulder while I read or did my homework. I saw another world through the eyes of my kestrel. It was a world of crickets, meadow flowers, cumulus clouds, thunderheads, and tree hollows.

Now my children would know that world.

The day Iliad arrived, Crowbar flew to his apple tree, turned his back, and ignored him. This was odd, because crows are born to harass falcons, owls, and hawks with gusto and verve. Crowbar preened, so I assumed he was so imprinted on his human family that he did not recognize a falcon as an enemy. I was wrong.

Karen made a perch for Iliad. She covered a cylinder of wood with leather to protect his feet and ran an iron rod into the wood block. She put a steel ring on the ground and pushed the perch into it. John had already put the falconers' jesses and a leash on Iliad, so Karen had only to tie the leash to the iron ring to keep him from flying away. He sat quietly, bobbing his head and taking in his surroundings.

We had a falcon in our midst, that regal bird of kings and monarchs. The blue jays screamed

at him and the robins clicked their alarm note. Then Hands came loping across the yard, saw Iliad, and, head-down, ears back, charged him playfully. Iliad flew to the end of his leash and dropped to earth. Craig grabbed Hands and Karen picked up Iliad.

"That's a good lesson for us," I said. "We'd better not put Iliad outdoors unless there's someone around to watch him."

I looked for Crowbar, still thinking he might harass him. He was not to be seen.

For several days Iliad was the center of attention. At almost any time of the day I could look out my sunporch windows and see one or another of the children seated several yards from Iliad, whistling to him and holding food in their hands. We had devised a whistle of three notes that meant "come for food." It did not take long for Iliad to learn to fly from his perch to the hand and, after a while, to fly all the way across the yard to us.

Sometimes Luke would sit beside his perch and watch everything the falcon watched: a bee, a twisting leaf, the flight of the red-shouldered hawk overhead. He saw a myriad of things that he had never seen before. Remembering my childhood, I smiled. The little falcon was taking Luke with him into his world.

One day when I put Iliad outside, I heard the phone ring and went indoors to answer it. When I came out, Iliad was gone. The perch was lying on the ground. In my haste I had not pushed it into the soil far enough. It had fallen, and Iliad had taken off with leash and ring. I was devastated. The ring would catch somewhere and hold him until he died.

Frantically I searched the nearby tree limbs. He was nowhere to be seen.

Crowbar alit on the picnic table.

"Hey, fellow," I said. "Where have you been lately?" I hurried into the house to get Karen to help me find the falcon.

"He can't be far with that leash and iron ring," she said, following me into the backyard. I glanced at Crowbar. He had walked to the edge of the table and was fluttering his wings and lifting his feathers, begging for attention—but I had no time for him.

Karen and I turned and ran up the hill through the woods, whistling the three notes that should bring Iliad home. All was still; not even the blue jays screamed. We wove back and forth among the trees and bushes. As the hours wore on I grew heartsick. Iliad did not stand a chance if we did not find him today or tomorrow.

When the kids came home from school, we widened the search. Craig went into nearby yards, Twig took the roads, and Luke went down to the swamp; but there was no sign of Iliad.

We hunted until almost dark, then came home for a supper of warmed-over soup.

"Hello," said Crowbar from the sill of the kitchen window.

"He hasn't said that for a while," said Craig.

Crowbar wiped his beak on the sill, then hopped to the floor. He leaned against Luke's foot.

"He's being awful cute," Luke said, and petted him.

After dinner Karen and I made plans for a pre-sunrise search; then reluctantly I walked to the telephone. "I've got to tell your dad," I said, and dialed my brother.

"That's not the first time that's happened," he said. "It has happened to the best of the falconers, but it's always sad."

He gave me some suggestions as to how to go about finding him. With heavy heart I put down the phone and glanced out the window. Something moved near the top of the window. Crowbar was leaning down into the light beam watching me. I chuckled. He was not only a toy thief but a spy.

Then my suspicions flowered.

"What have you learned from your spying?" I asked out loud. "Do you know when the phone rings I will go into the house and answer it? Do you know that I am fastened to that phone for several minutes to many? Do you know that when I say, 'Okay, good-bye,' I'll be free to walk about again?"

I went on. "Did you dive-bomb the falcon when I was talking on the phone? Did you know he could fly no farther than the end of the leash? Did you know he would then fall to the ground and you could attack him?

"But that didn't happen, did it? Instead, the perch, which I had not pushed far enough into the ground, toppled over at his frantic pull when you dive-bombed him; and he was off with leash and ring. Is that how it happened?

"Crowbar, did you know what you were doing? Did you?"

I thought so. And I still do.

CHAPTER 11

The Robin in a Teacup and the Chickadee in the Sunporch

Not all birds are as clever as Crowbar. Some are simply sweet children of instinct. And every spring brought new wild orphans to adopt. Lost baby robins are eternally delightful and were always welcomed to our house.

Every May and June children find baby robins on the ground fluttering their wings to say, "I am hungry, take care of me." Children never fail to understand that message. They pick them up and bring them home.

That day or maybe the next, I will get a phone call from frantic parents asking me if I will take the robins.

They arrive in shoe boxes, Kleenex nests, and warm cupped hands. If they are in good condition, I tell the child and parents to return the bird to the place where they found it. "Wait two hours," I advise. "If the parents do not appear and feed it, then there are no parents. Bring it back."

Pete was one of those who came back. He was a small half-feathered little bird in a shoe box, with blue pin feathers, a big yellow mouth, and bleary eyes. He looked as if he were not going to make it. We gave him water in an eyedropper and a bit of canned dog food mixed with calcium and vitamins. When he stopped eating, Craig put him back in the box and put it on the kitchen drainboard, where we all could take turns feeding him.

"We have to feed Pete every twenty minutes. Wherever you are, if you hear him calling, come feed him. The food's here in the refrigerator. Warm it in your hand before you give it to him."

All that day Craig and Twig responded to Pete's call for food. Luke dug worms for him in the compost heap.

Despite the tender care, Pete did not look well at nightfall. I prepared myself to awaken early before the kids and bury him. I put a heating pad under his shoe box—for it was a cool night—covered the box with a towel, and went to bed.

At five A.M. Twig woke me up when she stepped on the squeaky floorboard in her room, on her way to look at Pete. I slipped downstairs with her.

Pete was very much alive. In the soft light of daybreak he was screaming for food, mouth wide open. Twig warmed the food in her hands and stuffed him until he was quiet.

At lunchtime Pete was snuggled in a teacup on the table. His head shot up like a jack-in-the-box when anyone sat down. Even a jiggle on the floor would set him frantically begging for food. Movements, shadows, vibrations, all were "parents." We worked like a chain gang to keep him fed.

Pete lived that day, another day, and another. By the end of the week he was covered with feathers and had a full complement of stubby wing feathers. His breast was spotted. Pete was a handsome and healthy baby robin.

One morning Twig brought him in his cup to the dining-room table. But no sooner had she set the cup down than he was out of it. Two feet together, he hopped from child to child. When he got to Luke, he was scooped up in both hands and pressed gently under his chin.

"I'm going to take him back to his mother," he said.

"No, you're not," Craig answered. "He's mine."

"No, he's not. He's his mother's."

Twig got into it. "Why don't you take Boay back to his mother if you're so anxious to get babies back to their moms?" Boay was Luke's snake.

"Boay doesn't need a mom," said Luke. "As soon as he was born, he could slither away from home and find food. He found it with his tongue and the heat sensor on his head. He could catch little mice with his mouth, squeeze them to death with his body, and swallow them whole. He has forty-seven ribs."

"Listen to our little brother," said Twig, her eyes widening. "Mom, listen to Luke. He's talking whole paragraphs from the encyclopedia."

Luke had been a quiet little boy until fourth grade. We did not realize it, but all that time he was carefully observing his older brother and sister and learning from their mistakes. He saw that it was better to do your homework than not, better to put your toys away than leave them out to get broken, and better to read. And read he did. On that Saturday morning when he gave his first information-packed lecture on boa constrictors, we knew that the quiet little boy was a force to be reckoned with.

Craig was not be diverted by snake tales.

"We can't take Pete back to his mom," he said, "because we don't know where she is."

"Besides," said Twig, "he likes us."

That seemed to settle it for Craig and her, but not for Luke. A little later in the day he opened the door and coaxed Pete into the sunshine with a worm. When he thought Pete was free, he went inside. A few minutes later, Pete was inside.

Try as he would, Luke could not make him go. Pete's inner clock was ticking along the course of robin development—from a blind naked screamer who could only lift its head and open its mouth to a competent and independent adult. He could not be hurried along to what we thought was freedom.

When Pete was in the fledgling stage, he worked out a fledgling routine for himself in our house. Early in the morning after the kids had fed him breakfast, he would hop into my workroom. I would pick him up and put him on the windowsill. From there he could flutter up onto the spout of the watering can and take a good firm hold on the spout. From this airy perch the garden outside was visible to him if he looked in one direction, and my typewriter if he looked in the other.

There on the watering-can spout, well fed and safe from harm, he would sleep. After an hour he would awaken and chirp and one or another of us would let him perch on a finger. At this stage he held fast to finger, stick, watering-can spout—no matter where the kids put him. After his meal he would sleep again. This went on until the twilight darkened to night and he would be put in his shoe box to be carried upstairs to Twig's pillow.

When he could fly, he graduated to the pre-teens. He was both independent and dependent. He went out the door, enjoyed the garden, but always came back to be fed and comforted. At this stage he was a beautiful friend.

In July he brought me a chickadee. It happened this way: On a warm afternoon Pete flew in through the sunporch door and perched on the watering can. Suddenly, with a whir and a flash of black and white feathers, a chickadee followed him in. The bold adventurer hovered in the air in front of my face, scolding me severely. I saw that the bird feeder was empty and picked up a sun-flower seed from the feed bag and held it between my fingers. The pretty bird hovered over my hand and, still on wing, took the offering in his beak. He sped out the door to the apple tree. There he held

the seed with his toes and cracked it open with his
beak. He ate, wiped his beak clean, and flew back
in the door. I picked up another seed. This time he
alit on my fingers, his tiny feet feeling cool and
weightless. His black eye glistened as he tipped his
head and looked at me. I was enchanted. I had

heard that chickadees come to know the people who live on their territories and will eat out of their hands, but this was the first time it had happened to me. We named him Parus, from *Parus atricapillus*, the Latin name for the black-capped chickadee.

Parus came back often to take seeds from my fingers. I would hear a *whirr* of wings and there he would be, hovering near my head waiting for a seed or two. He must have enjoyed this contact, for after the first time there was always food in the bird feeder when he came to me. A couple of sunflower seeds could not have been the sole reward. I like to think I was Parus's pet human. People need pets, so why wouldn't other animals?

While Parus and his mate were raising a second brood of chicks in the wren box on the oak tree, we saw little of him. But in August, when the young were on their own, he was back in the sunporch, daintily taking seeds from my hand.

Meanwhile the nights were growing longer and the migrating birds were responding to the shorter hours of daylight. Declining light trips their migratory triggers, and some are on their way by late August.

There was a wild restlessness in Pete by mid-September. Not Parus. He was a resident bird, one of those who, unlike the migratory birds, stays on the same property winter, spring, summer, and fall. His young raised, he now had the leisure time to come into the sunporch and tarry awhile. He was growing tamer and tamer with the changes in the light, while Pete was growing wilder.

Luke and I were picking up apples one day in late September, and Pete was chasing bees who were gathered on the lemonade pitcher. Suddenly he flew to the mock orange bush. Something about his flight had struck a familiar note.

"*Clink,*" he chirped.

"Pete's grown up," I said to Luke, "and he's going to go off and seek his fortune. He's going to leave us. He's calling the note of the migrating robin."

Pete flew to the apple tree. He turned his head as he took a reading on the polarized light rays of the sun. He hopped higher into the tree. For many minutes he sat there, a slender, intense bird, interpreting signals from the atmosphere. Then he flew.

The sun had called him south and west. Pete was on his own.

CHAPTER 12

A Crow Kidnapping

Crowbar stayed. Two and a half years had passed since he had joined the family. After Pete left, he strutted down to the bus stop on school days, kept me company, and flew to the middle school at noon to call on his moneyed friends.

One morning as the sun was coming up, I heard crows yelling from my trees and yard. I ran to the window. Thirty or forty of the big black birds, who were on migration, were gathered on limbs, lawn, and picnic table. They were directing their caws at Crowbar.

"You're a crow. You're a crow. Come with us," I was certain they were saying. Crows do not like to see their kind become pet crows.

I tried to pick out Crowbar from the mob, but could not. They all looked alike. This was embarrassing, since Crowbar would fly right to my shoulder when I got off the train. He could find me in a mass of humans, but I could not find him in a crowd of crows.

The kids awoke, and we hung out the windows watching the drama below.

"He's going to go away with them," said Luke when the chorus rose to a frantic pitch.

"Get the hamburger," Twig said, and she and Craig dashed downstairs. Before they returned, the sun had flooded the hillside with light and the crows had taken off. Sitting alone was Crowbar. We ran outside and fed him until he could eat no more.

"Crows do know a good thing when they see it," said Luke, glad the family crow had stayed.

The next morning the birds returned. Crows are very sensible migrants. None of this flying fifteen thousand miles from the Arctic to the tip of South America and then back again, as some birds do, or for that matter even from New York to Florida. Crows migrate only as far as their favorite winter roosting sites, which can be no more than twenty miles away.

The telephone rang the third morning of the crow visitation.

"What are all the crows doing here?" asked Art Buckley, who lived at the bottom of the hill. "I've never, in all the twenty years I've lived here, seen so many crows." Then he added, "They wake me up at five. What can we do about it?"

"Wait," I said. "They'll go away."

I was not sure about that. I had never had a massive gang of crows come to abduct a pet. What would happen if they all came to recognize a good thing when they saw it and stayed on too?

On the fifth day we heard a new note in the communal voice of the crows. It was an unmistakable jubilation. Excitement infused their cacophony. Craig sped down to the refrigerator for food.

He got back in time to see the crows take off. They beat their black taffeta wings and flew up over our trees and down the valley—and there was no more Crowbar.

Despite our tears, it was a beautiful ending to a wild-pet story.

CHAPTER 13

The Boa Constrictor and the Nancy Drew Club

"Go look at Luke's room," Twig said to Craig several days after they came home from summer camp. "Things are evolving there."

Craig opened the door. "Wow!" he said, and started counting:

> 1 black snake
> 1 king snake
> 1 iguana
> 1 horned toad
> 2 box turtles
> 1 gypsy moth in a cocoon
> 7 salamanders
> 12 toad tadpoles
> 7 bullfrog tadpoles
> and 1 boa constrictor

Boay was now almost four feet long and as thick as my wrist. He was sleek and handsome. Usually he was coiled quietly in his big glass aquarium under his sun lamp, but this day he was weaving around the enclosure, sliding up the sides and poking at the lid.

"He's hungry," Twig said, and fetched Luke.

"I'll feed him," he told her, and went to the basement for one of the white rats he raised for Boay.

"Don't feed him until I call the Nancy Drew Club," said Twig. "I promised they could come over the next time you gave him a rat."

"Well, tell them to hurry," said Luke. "He's real hungry, and you know what that means."

"Yeah," said Craig. "He'll knock the lid off his cage, get out, and scare the Nancy Drew Club senseless."

Boay did get out more often than I like to remember. When he did, we'd close all the doors and search for him. Once we found him under the covers on Twig's bed, and twice Virginia Wiggins, my invaluable helper and second mother to the kids, discovered him in the clothes basket. Most employees would have quit the first time that happened.

Boay was not about to get out, and Twig called the Nancy Drew Club. Three of the six teenagers appeared at the door. One had just ironed her hair straight on the ironing board, as was the rage that year, and it gleamed like a metal sheet.

Debbie, Jessica, Ellie, and Twig gathered in Luke's room in chattering expectation. Craig sensed drama and came to the doorway. When all the girls were in, Luke held the white rat by its tail and opened the lid—and Boay was out.

Screaming girls hugged each other. Luke was about to grab him when he turned and headed for the bed. The screams became wilder.

"Drop the rat to him," Craig said. Luke did, and Boay felt the heat from the rodent, who was also headed for the bed. Boay snatched it in his jaws and, using his body like a hand, took it from his mouth and placed it in a coil.

Slowly Boay tightened the coil. The rat made no protest as its life was squeezed away. Researchers have found that the animals snakes prey upon are as good as dead and incapable of moving when the snake stares at them. I watched a frog in the woods in Michigan sit stone still while a snake, eyes upon it, slid right up to it and took it in its mouth. The frog never moved to safety.

When the rat was dead, Boay opened his mouth and unhinged the bones in his jaw so that he could open it as wide as the rat was. Then, his body behaving like a hand again, he put the food daintily in his mouth—headfirst.

The Nancy Drew Club was riveted with horror and fascination as slowly, slowly the rat disappeared, head, shoulders, hips, and lastly tail. On their knees now, they watched the rat lump move down the long body to the stomach. Luke picked up the now docile Boay and put him back in the glass aquarium.

"That's how he eats," he said.

"Yeah," said Craig. "That's how he eats."

The girls were quiet; then Ellie spoke up. "Who needs Nancy Drew?" she said, and jumped off the bed. "She's a real bore after Boay."

Ellie became an environmentalist.

CHAPTER 14

The White Mouse Experiment

While Boay ate rats and got lost in the house, Twig took on a project for science class.

"I'm going to study two white mice," she informed me one day. "I'll keep notes on what they do. Notes are the secret of scientific investigation, my teacher said."

"True," I answered. We went to the pet shop for mice, cage, wheel, food and water dispenser, and two white mice she named Dick and Jane.

"What are you hoping to discover?" I asked her.

"The notes will reveal it. You're not supposed to have an answer before you begin, or you'll influence the conclusion."

"True," I answered.

We took Dick and Jane home, and the experiment, whatever it was, began.

Twig George—White Mouse Experiment

March 12, 1964

Dick and Jane sniffed the cage and made a nest in the oatmeal box. They ran in the wheel.

March 24

Jane bit Dick; then she had six babies. As soon as they were all born, Dick mated with Jane. The babies are pink, hairless, blind, and not real pretty.

March 28

The babies are cute. Their eyes are open. Their names are Mary, Ann, Bill, Charlie, Fred, and Priscilla. Craig said Boay likes baby mice. I chased him out of the room.

April 3

Jane had six more babies. Their names are Jack, Moe, Kate, Ellen, Helen, Buster. Dick mated with Jane.

April 14

Jane had five more babies. She had them in the wheel. Their names are Henry . . .

May 12

Mary is pregnant.

May 14

Mary had six babies. So did Priscilla.

There are *twenty-five* white mice. They fight a lot. They eat a lot of food and the cage smells. I have to clean it every day instead of once a week.

May 30

I think Jane, Mary, Priscilla, and some other female had litters of four to six babies in the wheel, and I can't tell who is who. There must be *fifty* white mice in the cage. The babies are getting stepped on. Ugh.

June 1

Jane and Mary are eating their babies. This is awful. The whole cage is a wiggling mass of pink, raw babies half eaten. More are on the way. This is a revolting experiment.

I heard Twig running down the steps.

"I can't look in the mouse cage anymore," she cried. "It's horrible, it's awful. What should I do?"

"It's time to get rid of them," I said. "Would you like to keep Dick and Jane?"

"No."

"Do you have a conclusion for your experiment?" I asked.

"Revolting," she said.

Boay ate well, and Twig never discussed her experiment again.

End of experiment.

CHAPTER 15

The Skunk in the Closet

Virginia was also happy to see the mice go. She was smiling the day the cage went to the basement. With a thank-goodness-that's-over sigh, she opened Twig's windows wide and let the fresh air from the woods blow through the room.

Then Craig came home with a baby skunk.

We made a den for him in Craig's closet and took turns feeding him from a baby bottle. Mason was stunning. He had two white stripes down his back. The black and white plumes on his tail, short as they were, cascaded over his back like an elegant shawl when he lifted his tail.

After a few days Craig was Mom. When he came home from school, Mason would clatter across the floor, his long digging claws tapping out a tattoo, and greet him with a throaty chitter.

Craig would pick him up and stroke the white cap on his black head, and the little skunk would cuddle against him. Mason, I told him, was going to be as delightful a pet as my first pet skunk, Meph (for *Mephitis mephitis*, the scientific name for the American striped skunk).

Meph lived with John and me at the tent in the Michigan woods where he and I camped for four years while he studied the birds of the area for his Ph.D. Meph was more like a cat than any other mammal I had raised. He kept close to us, slept in a box under the table, liked to sit in our laps, and grew fat and lazy on his favorite food, chili con carne.

Nothing disturbed Meph. He walked the forest

floor with the confidence of the skunk. The great horned owls could fly overhead, the fox could pass in the night, but Meph trod methodically on, neither fleeing nor seeking shelter. That black-and-white warning message he wore read, "Do not mess," and held all enemies at spray's length.

Meph never sprayed. It is not true that you need to remove the scent glands from a pet skunk to make it livable. Skunks just don't spray unless their lives are threatened. Like the crows, skunks know a good thing when they see it, and for Meph, it was a warm lap and chili con carne.

But there can be tense moments when a pet skunk is not descented. At the same time we had Meph, we had Lotor's two yearling raccoons. They were a frolicsome pair and liked to include Meph in their roughhousing. When he came out of his warm box, they would prance before him and roll and tumble him. Sweet-dispositioned Meph took as much of this as he could, then he would throw up his tail to spray. The raccoons would jump on his tail and pull it down.

To this day I wonder how they knew a skunk could only spray when its tail was up.

Luke was at the apex of his Animal Freedom Movement when we acquired Mason. He had opened his window one morning and let our young white-throated sparrow fly to freedom, and returned two baby gray squirrels to the foot of the tree where they had been born. Now he had his eye on Mason.

One day when Luke was in Craig's room, Virginia came into the room to clean, looked into the closet where Mason was sleeping, and gave a deep sigh. Luke came downstairs. "Virginia doesn't like Mason," he said.

I was jolted to my senses. Virginia and I were very close. We had been divorced about the same time, and her problems were mine, mine hers. We had laughed about the wild animals we had both nurtured as children, and so it had never occurred to me that a skunk in a closet might bother Virginia. Luke was right: I had not been very considerate of her.

Craig and I moved Mason to the toolshed. Here he was sheltered but free to come and go. Without looking back, he disappeared among the flowerpots and old hand mowers. There was a shuffling of objects, then silence. We listened for several minutes, then put a bowl of dog food and a bowl of water outside the door and went back to the house.

At dusk we were happy to see Mason come out of hiding and feast. He investigated the daylily garden, dug for insect larvae in the lawn, then waddled up the hill. We thought of the dangers ahead: two roads, a German shepherd's property, and several kids with BB guns. It was not a very good environment for a skunk. Not knowing all this, Mason plodded confidently along and vanished into the night.

"He's gone forever," said Craig, his voice wistful.

But he wasn't. Every evening Mason would come out of the toolshed and eat. Then he would wander through the garden and up the hill. The dog did not chase him, the cars stopped for him, and the kids with the BB guns never saw him. Maybe, we thought, our neighborhood is safe for a skunk.

The evening came when we did not see Mason. A week and finally months passed, and then it appeared that Craig was right. Our neighborhood had not been a good environment for a skunk.

We could not have been more incorrect. Unbeknownst to him, Morty Ross, who lives down the hill, now has a skunk family in his backyard. Al Bachman has one under his woodpile, and uphill under a brush pile in Marcy Reid's woods is another. Mason and his descendants did very well.

CHAPTER 16

Learning from a Box Turtle

One autumn day when Luke was releasing a box turtle in the woods at the Teatown Reservation, a woman asked him why he had kept such a pet.

"I learned a lot," he said.

"Keeping a box turtle in captivity is learning a lot?" she asked not unkindly, but uncomprehendingly.

Luke explained that he now knew how turtles eat and tap each other on the back to chat.

Luke learned something else about a box turtle, and so did I.

He kept Boxy in his room upstairs, and because Luke was reentering his Animal Freedom Movement period, Boxy was free to traipse around his room. One night he wandered into the hall and I heard him walking toward the steps. Luke heard him too, and we met in the hall to save him from falling down the stairs. Then I reasoned aloud.

"Turtles come to cliffs in the woods," I said to Luke. "They must sense the open space below them and turn back. After all, they have survived for hundreds of thousands of years. They must know all about cliffs. Let's go to sleep."

So we did.

Then *crash, bang, thump, bang, bang, bang,* Boxy fell all the way down the steps to the landing. I jumped out of bed.

"That ought to teach him," said Luke, who had joined me. "He won't fall down the next steps." While we spoke, Boxy walked across the landing and fell down the next flight. Then he tromped off across the foyer.

"Turtles fall," said Luke. "Now we know that."

We also learned that box turtles are intelligent. They recognize you and will come when you call them to food. They also make wonderful pets for young children with their hard armor and docile dispositions. The best turtles are those native to your part of the world, for when the child has learned what he can from having a turtle, you can let it walk back to its own world, none the worse for the wear.

CHAPTER 17

The Bat in the Refrigerator

Another pet from which we learned wondrous bits of knowledge was a bat. Sonar, Craig named her.

We came across her in winter. Sonar had been hibernating under the bark of a tree, but the tree was felled and lay on the ground. She had been jolted from her home and, in her hibernating state, could not find another. She was cold, motionless, and deep in sleep. We knew she could never find a new hideout in that condition, so we brought her home. The kids walled a cardboard box with a piece of carpeting and hung Sonar on it. She clung by her tiny claws. I placed her gently in the refrigerator. We planned to keep her there until spring. In her dormancy she would be a nice pet. We would not even have to feed her, just admire her and keep her cold.

Of course, the inevitable happened. Someone took Sonar out of the refrigerator to show her off and did not put her back. When I came home from a research trip, she was winging around the living room in the springlike temperature of the house.

"She can go right through the hula hoop," Twig said, holding it up, "and never touch it anywhere."

"And she can miss the chandelier."

"And hang on the little plaster bumps on the wall."

Virginia, who had been baby-sitting, came into the room and sat down.

"This has been an interesting time," she said, and chuckled.

"How are we going to feed her now that she's awake?" I asked the kids. "She eats insects, and it's winter."

"Crickets," Luke answered. "From the pet shop. You said you tossed crickets to a bat you had when Twig was a baby. We could do that."

"We'll spill cake crumbs on the floor and the ants will come," said Twig. "Sonar can eat the ants like Toad did."

Virginia wisely observed, "That bat likes to rest on rough things. We could hang a bunch of towels around, and when she stops on one, we'll wrap her up in it and take her to the attic. It's cold up there."

"You're right," I said.

"Neat," said Twig. "Bats belong in attics."

Two days later we finally caught Sonar and released her in the attic among the books, drums, electric guitars, and the outgrown dollhouse. As I turned back the folds of the towel, we all got a good look at a magical bat. Sonar opened her mouth, and we imagined the inaudible sounds that she was sending out to locate herself. Her ears were large receiving discs. Her eyes were small in a furry head. She could see so well with her ears that she did not have to see well with her eyes. Her wings and tail were like the webbing in Goose's feet. With the tail and wings she caught and ate insects while flying.

"Nature can sure make up some unreal creatures," said Virginia.

"Let her go," said Luke.

She flew to a rafter and hooked her wing claws in a knothole, turned around, and hung upside down by her feet. I opened the window a crack.

"She'll 'hear' the opening in the window with her sonar," I said, "and will leave when the weather is right."

"Granddad told me," said Craig, "that once you get bats in the attic, you can't get them out. They drop their scent to tell other bats to join them. They drop more stuff, and more bats join them. Pretty soon you have hundreds and hundreds of bats in the attic, like at Granddad's house in Pennsylvania."

"When Sonar's gone," said Luke, "we'll close the window."

CHAPTER 18

The Tarantula in My Purse

"Crickets for the tarantula" was an item on my grocery list for almost seven years. I had found her crossing the highway in Oklahoma while I was doing the research for *One Day in the Prairie*, one of five tales about natural ecosystems.

My wonderful friend Ellan Young, a photographer-artist who photographs children and wildlife, had come with me on the trip. We had camped for ten days meeting bison, prairie dogs, rattlesnakes, and gorgeous huge furry tarantulas as big as a man's hand. Now we were driving to the airport to return home when Taran the tarantula walked out on the road into heavy traffic.

"Stop the car," Ellan said. "She'll never make the crossing. We've got to save her." I pulled off the road. Ellan stopped the traffic while I scooped up the great spider and put her in a plastic bag and then placed her in my purse.

I handled my purse very carefully all the way home.

Tarantulas are like Humpty Dumpty. When they fall, they smash. The thin, shell-like carapace that protects the large, watery abdomen cannot be put back together again. I was relieved when I got her home and into a terrarium.

She came to be tolerant of us, if not friendly, and would climb onto our hands and, on cold days, sit in the warmth of a palm. It is a myth that the bite of a tarantula is fatal, although some people react to a tarantula's bite more than others.

"Taran has never bitten anyone," I heard Luke explain to a friend who had asked the inevitable question. "So we don't know if we'll die."

About twice a year Taran molted her exoskeleton when she grew too big for her old one. We knew it was about to happen when she stopped eating for two or three days. Next the luster would leave her eyes as the old chitin separated from the new, and the metamorphosis began. We would try to be on hand for this remarkable performance, but only once did we get there on time.

The back split, and slowly, slowly, as if stepping out of a glass form, she would squeeze her eight feet, every hair, every antenna, every mouth part, scale, and joint. Then she would thrash violently as she extricated herself. Presently she was standing outside her old skin.

On the sand at the bottom of the terrarium there would be two identical images—one was Taran, and one was her old self. The old selves could be picked up and handled, and by the time Luke went off to college, he had several old selves in his room to startle his classmates.

Inspired by Taran, Craig created his most famous sign one September day. He nailed it to the tree at the end of the walk. Twig was at Bennington College, he was enrolled at Utah

State University, and Luke was about to go to Reed College. I would be home alone. Craig thought I might need protection.

"Beware of the Tarantula," it read.

CHAPTER 19

The Magpie Dilemma

The children did not stop collecting pets when they entered college. Luke took the tarantula exoskeletons to college, and Craig came home with a magpie. Like every pet magpie I have known, she was called Maggie.

Maggie had much of the savvy of Crowbar. She came by it naturally. Magpies are members of the same family, the Corvidae, as the crows and jays. She, like all magpies, was a jester in regal clothing, with her iridescent purple head and long, graceful green tail and wings. White epaulets and a white belly band gave her the look of a well-groomed royal prince—but she stole, ate birds' eggs, danced for her supper, and garbled a querulous nasal *maaaag*. When none of this got the attention she needed, she flew off to the neighbors'.

Children screaming and clapping uphill beyond

the woods meant Maggie had arrived and she was being fed cake and cookies.

One day she did not return, and Craig went off on a magpie hunt. He loved that bird. She had not only gotten him through his college exams by staying up with him all night sitting on his shoulder, but she would ride on his bike and on Saturday nights sit on his knee and listen to him play the guitar and sing.

"It was true love," his roommate agreed.

In midmorning the next day the radio presenter who reported lost and found pets read this: "A large black-and-white bird with a long iridescent tail was found." She gave a phone number.

We did not hear the announcement, but a

friend of Craig's did and called him the next day. Craig dialed the woman.

"You say the bird is yours?" the woman asked. "A man just came to the house and said it was his. He even knew what it was: a white-shouldered raven from India."

Then Craig's childhood friend Melissa Young called. Melissa was the one who could always save a wild animal. She had raised to adults two little cottontail rabbits that were almost dead when she found them. She had raised tiny baby wrens, been hired by the Bronx Zoo as a teenager to work with the camels in their children's zoo, and had almost as many dogs and cats as we had had.

"Guess what I've got?" she said.

"I can't," said Craig.

"A white-shouldered raven from India."

"Oh no," said Craig. "I'm coming right over."

The man who had picked up Maggie was, we should have all guessed, a Mount Kisco pet-store owner, who was famous for finding and reselling lost pets. He had charged Melissa fifty dollars for Maggie, dollars she had been saving for many months.

The pet-store owner would not give Melissa her money back, and so the problem became who owned Maggie. Melissa thought she was Craig's; Craig felt she was Melissa's.

While they were trying to find a solution, Cousin Charlie called from Moose, Wyoming, asking Craig to come out for the summer.

"Take Maggie back to her home," Melissa said happily. "That will solve everything. Maggie belongs to Maggie."

"Right," said Luke. Luke, of course, had returned all his pets to the wild and now kept only Taran's old selves.

Craig gave Maggie back to the wild.

CHAPTER 20

Filling the Empty Nest

One summer day, while visiting the Craighead homestead in Pennsylvania, I stopped to see my friend Jean Bixler. Her redbrick house sits on a shaded street in Boiling Springs and is surrounded by gardens and walks. I paused at the gate to admire her flowers, then went up the back steps.

Bobwhite, bobwhite, bobwhite, I heard from the house. *Bob, Bob White*. Running to the door came Cracker, a northern bobwhite quail. He lifted his crest and drooped his wings and lifted his head to threaten me.

"It's all right, Cracker," Jean said, and picked him up.

Cracker not only defended her house and garden but called a soft "come here" whistle to Jean when he found a delightful bug in the garden he wanted her to share with him. He also awoke her at dawn with his bright, melodic call, warned her of strangers, and announced friends.

I have a great fondness for birds. They are mysterious wonders. How did they come to fly? What is the language they speak with their beautiful colors that say "follow me" or "hide" when flashed?

Birds are not my captives; I am a captive of theirs. All are fascinating, but after meeting Cracker, I wanted a bird with the social graces of Jean Bixler's northern bobwhite, *Colinus virginianus*. I wanted a bobwhite to defend the house with song and raise feathers when strangers appeared.

The best way to get one, I decided, was to buy an incubator and hatch him myself.

About five miles from Chappaqua a bird-dog trainer named Leon raised bobwhites. I went to his home to get *one* egg.

"You've gotta take twelve to get one," he said. "Not all the eggs hatch."

So I took twelve eggs home and, of course, twelve eggs hatched.

As they hatched, I put them under a light until they were fluffy and dry. The petite dozen fit into a glass soup bowl while I cleaned the nursery box, and at the sight of the pretty patterns on the hatchlings repeated over and over again, I was smitten.

I could not pick the one I wanted. I wanted them all.

Hours later I was being followed by twelve little bobwhites. By the end of the day they were looking at each other more than they were at me. I had to decide at once which one to keep or it would not imprint on me. I picked one up, held it close to my face, stroked its pretty head, and put it down. Then I picked up another. This went on all day.

During the night two got into a fight and one killed the other. Two more refused to eat and died in the afternoon. Maybe, I thought, I won't have to decide which one to keep, and so I let the time of imprinting run out.

Seven bobwhites lived through the first two weeks. The genetically weak had been eliminated, and because I couldn't decide which one to keep, I raised seven bobwhites.

They did not call to me to share food, but they did announce the red-shouldered hawk that appeared the day I put them outside in a pen. And they did announce the sunrise with their flutelike *bobwhite*.

When they were two months old, they let me into their secret of survival. Bobwhites form coveys. At night these coveys sit in circles with their tails in and their heads out so that they may see or hear the enemy in all directions.

First I noticed two little chicks standing close to each other when they ate. They walked side by side. Two others teamed up, and one of the last independent three joined the first pair. This seemed to stimulate the others, and they clustered.

By the end of the month they were a covey. They walked, all heads pointing in the same direction, and they constantly kept in touch with each other with little chirps and peeps. At night they began to roost heads out, in a circle of feathers.

I spent many thoughtful hours watching the advantages of the covey. The little birds warned of the hawk, they called each other to buds and bugs, and they scratched the ground and found delicious things for each other. And I was on the outside of their circle.

A house sparrow named Darwin soon took the place of the devoted bobwhite I would never have. I found him naked on the sidewalk at the train station and he imprinted on me. Before I knew it, I had a little bird that not only defended the house but built nests for me. Cracker had never built a nest for Jean. Darwin built many—in the bookcases, on the mantelpiece, and in the leaves and stems of the houseplants.

Darwin particularly loved to fly into the long hair of the young men of the 1970s and start nesting. I told Louis Untermeyer, a friend and renowned poet, about Darwin. Louis wanted to meet him. He also wanted to meet Craig, who had made me a poetic license complete with a hand-drawn New York State stamp and a list of things the license permitted me to do. One was to ignore bad literary reviews. Louis thought he needed one of Craig's poetic licenses, too, so we invited him and his wife, Bryna, to dinner.

Louis, a man of impeccable taste, arrived for the evening dressed in a gray suit with a pale-blue shirt and a beautiful Pucci tie. It was knotted loosely in the style of the day.

We were no sooner seated at the table than Darwin left his nest on the mantel and flew right into the knot on Louis's tie.

"I'll take him out," I said, rising.

"No, no," replied Louis. "He's charming. I've never had a sparrow in my tie. This is quite an honor."

But I worried all during dinner. How was I going to extricate Darwin? He became very aggressive when anyone tried to remove him from one of his nests, and this expensive tie, apparently, was the best nest of all. He had not come out of it since going in. Now and then he stuck his beak out to make sure no one was going to take his property from him.

The meal came to an end. Now what to do?

We watched in horror as Louis reached for the bird. Darwin pecked him violently. Louis tried again. Darwin pecked five times rapidly. A note of defiance rang out from the necktie when Louis tried once more to remove him. Then Darwin struck him hard, three times in quick succession. Craig stared, Twig slid back in her chair and covered her eyes, and Luke got up to do something about the situation.

"How do I extricate him?" Louis asked with a chuckle.

"I don't know," Luke answered. "We've never had this problem before. We've never had a Pucci tie in this house."

"I guess there's only one solution," Louis said.

Loosening the tie, he pulled it over his head and handed Luke the beautiful tie and its tenant.

Darwin lived in the Pucci tie on the mantel until the day he flew out the door in pursuit of a female to share his elegant home with. Somehow he got lost in the great outdoors and never came back. The tie lay on the mantel until Craig learned that ties were required for a wedding he had to attend. Having none of his own, he took Louis Untermeyer's tie and did not put it back. I like to think he took it to college and wore it often, but I know better.

I brought Unca the fiddler crab back from a canoe trip in a Connecticut marsh and put him in a terrarium. He ate table scraps and dug caves and caverns in the mud I had provided for him.

Unca was a hit in the neighborhood. The young kids liked to come by and tap his glass container. Like a flash he would run out of his cave and raise his one huge claw over his face.

"He's defending his property," I would tell them. "Hold your finger horizontally in front of him, and he'll think you're another fiddler crab and charge you."

When the kids were no longer amused by Unca's bravado, I took him back to the marsh and put crab and mud back into the ocean wetland.

The house was empty but for an Airedale, Jill.

In late August and September I gather milkweed plants with monarch eggs on them and watch the eggs hatch and the larvae grow, turn into chrysalises, and emerge as gorgeous butterflies. Then I band them for the Urquardt Monarch Butterfly study at the University of Toronto and let them go. They face the southwest and start off on a migration that will take them 1,500 miles to the mountains near Mexico City.

One morning when I came in with eight monarch butterfly eggs on three milkweed stalks, I was met by a housefly. He alit on my shoulder and

rode into the kitchen with me. After noticing his gray body and crystal wings, I brushed him off and he flew off to some other perch.

That evening he reappeared in the kitchen and flew to the windowsill. He watched me toss a salad. I still paid him little heed, but when I sat down at the dining-room table and he joined me on the centerpiece, I felt called upon to speak to him.

"Hello, Buzzer," I said. "Are you following me?"

The next morning Buzzer was on the window-sill again, and as if answering me, he followed me to the dining-room table and sat on the center-piece.

"Have you come in for the winter to live with me?" I asked jokingly, but when in the afternoon he turned up on the dictionary on my desk, I began to wonder. I looked up *housefly* in the entomology book. I found that I had not a housefly but a wood fly, and that they did indeed come in for the winter and hibernate in the cracks and crevices of old barns and houses.

Buzzer grew slower and slower as the days passed, and he followed me from kitchen to dining room and dining room to front door. And then I saw him no more.

Perhaps he went out the door like the six monarch butterflies, or perhaps he overwintered in the woodwork. Wherever he was and whatever he was doing, I considered him the best pet. The day your house empties of children, you are not ready to take on anything larger than a fly.

CHAPTER 21

The Bullfrog Who Was a Prince

Twig and Craig and Luke are grown up now. Craig has two sons and is a biologist studying the bowhead whale in Barrow, Alaska. Twig has two daughters and a master's degree from the Bank Street College, and has written her first children's book, A *Dolphin Named Bob*. Luke is a Ph.D. in conservation biology and teaches at Humboldt College in Arcata, California.

Twig is married to David Pittenger, Director of the National Aquarium in Baltimore. Craig is married to Cyd, a public-health officer at the Barrow veterinary clinic. And Luke is married to Carol Ann Morehead, who has written two extraordinary children's books, *Backyard Wildlife* and *Wild Horses*.

We are all devoted to the natural world, and

when we get together, Twig, Craig, and Luke tell their spouses and children the stories of Yammer, Crowbar, Weasel, Goose, Duck, and their other wild pets. Everyone has a favorite pet.

Several Christmases ago Craig's wife, Cyd, asked me what my favorite pet was. Without hesitation I answered, "A bullfrog named Rana."

The bullfrog arrived in a bucket with eleven other bullfrogs that Craig and his friends had caught for the high school science teacher. "We're not going to dissect them," Craig told me. "The teacher's planning some behavioral study."

"Is it a frog-jumping contest?" I asked as I looked from the frogs to the young men. No one answered. Craig covered the bucket for the night. When the friends had traipsed off, I went to bed.

Around two in the morning I heard a pot lid clanking to the floor, and frogs croaking. I ran downstairs and turned on the lights. Frogs were hopping across the kitchen floor. Frogs were in the dining room, and frogs were in the foyer. They were very athletic, with good elevations and strides, but I managed to catch them and put them back in the bucket. This time I covered them with a heavy drawing board before I went back to bed.

At sunup I heard from the foyer below a deep melodious *Gu-rumphf*, *Gu-rumphf*, the mating song of *Rana catesbeiana*, the eastern bullfrog. One ingenious fellow had found the pool in the foyer and hopped in.

"Smart frog," I said to myself. "You are going to stay in our pond as long as you wish." I chuckled and dozed off to the sound of a summer dawn in the country—a bullfrog singing.

We named the frog Rana, and every evening that summer we would open the doors and windows to let the moths and summer insects come in to the lights. Then we would turn out the lights and go to bed. As I went off to sleep, I would hear Rana splat out of the pool and hop off around the house to catch the insects that had fallen to the floor.

That summer Twig was dating a young man I

really did not like. Twig's friends had always been my friends, but not this one. I had refrained from criticizing him, knowing how little good it would have done. One night Twig brought her friend to the house. He sat down in the living room while she went to the kitchen to get something to eat.

I heard the familiar splat that told me Rana was abroad.

With that, the living-room rocker squeaked and feet raced to the door. The door was yanked open and slammed closed, and footfalls clattered down the front walk. A car door opened and slammed shut. Stones clattered under spinning tires, and a car sped down the lane and was gone.

And we never saw that young man again.

"You see," I said to Cyd, "even a grandmother can have a frog prince."